FANTASY FLOWERS

Pieced Flowers for Quilters

**Doreen
Cronkite
Burbank**

That Patchwork Place®

Dedication

To Kathy Reader, without whom this book would never have been started, to Karen Senet, without whom it could never have been finished, and especially to my husband, Alan, who gave me world enough and time.

Acknowledgments and special thanks to:

Sandra Hatch, for thinking that I had something to offer to quilters.

Carol Babineau, for being talented, enthusiastic, and there when I needed her.

The Merrimack Valley Quilters who experimented with the early flower patterns: Cheryl Adam, Karla Cook, Connie Grew, Joan Ross, and Nancy Ryll.

Other quilters, among the many, who have given me inspiration: Ann Boyce, Carol Doak, Anne Gallo, Stephanie Hatch, Jean Hay, Ruth McDowell, Ruby Short McKim, Beth Schwartz, Susan Raban, and Sue Turbak.

All the exhibitors, members, and friends of the New England Quilt Museum.

My quilting foremothers: Virgiline Hanes Cronkite Wichelt, Hilda Hanes Powers Nauman, Bertha Williams Hanes, Amanda Williams, and Mary Smith Cronkite Wood.

My father, Henry O. Cronkite, who once made a quilt for his bed in college so he could have one that was long enough.

Credits

Photography	*Doug Plager*
Illustration & Graphics	*Doreen Burbank, Linda Campbell*
Text Design	*Connie Lunde*
Cover Design	*Judy Petry*
Editor	*Barbara Weiland*
Copy Editors	*Miriam Bulmer, Liz McGehee*

Fantasy Flowers: Pieced Flowers for Quilters©
©1992 by Doreen Cronkite Burbank

That Patchwork Place, Inc., PO Box 118, Bothell, WA 98041-0118

Printed in the Republic of Korea
97 96 95 94 93 92   6 5 4 3 2 1

Library of Congress Cataloging-in-Publication Data
Burbank, Doreen Cronkite
   Fantasy flowers: pieced flowers for quilters / Doreen Cronkite Burbank.
     p. cm.
   ISBN 1-56477-002-8:
   1. Patchwork–Patterns. 2. Flowers in art. 3. Appliqué–Patterns. 4. Machine appliqué.
I. Title.
TT835.B8 1992
746.46'041–dc20
                    91-44324
                    CIP

Published in the USA

CONTENTS

INTRODUCTION

The roots of this book lie in my long-held fantasy of making a flower quilt, despite my considerable shortcomings as a quilter: I do not like to piece by hand; I do not like to appliqué; and I do not like to work with curves. I'm just basically a lazy quilter who wants to make a great-looking project.

When I cook, I like to have the product look as if it had been a lot harder to make than it actually was. I prefer easy recipes that taste great and don't take as much time as they appear to. I like my "quilting recipes" the same way.

If you are the kind of quilter who delights in piecing a zillion tiny pieces by hand and spending two years finishing a quilt, we are not talking the same language here. This book is meant for those special people who: always wanted to make a flower quilt; know they couldn't appliqué a whole quilt top full of flowers in this lifetime; like to finish their projects before both they and the project turn gray; and believe that sewing machines were invented to make life easier.

"Quilting isn't hard to do if you remember that you started out to have fun."

Keep the Fun in Quilting

Quilting has become very popular around the world, and many, many people are involved in sewing together wonderful quilts. Not all of those people are any more clever than you and I. Not all of them have more free time than we could ever hope to have. Many of them have simply discovered the wonderful secret that quilting isn't hard to do if you remember that you started out to have fun! By eliminating some of the things that can make quiltmaking painfully slow, you can create many more projects without investing your life's blood in them.

Flower designs have always appealed to quilters, but most of the traditional flower blocks do not fit my "easy recipe" criteria. Real flowers are not straight-edged shapes, and they are definitely not formal arrangements of petals. Even the most perfect blossom has a bit of the random to it.

Using the patterns in this book, you can make quilt blocks that look like real flowers, even though they are made with straight edges and have a formal pattern. The key to making most of these blocks is the use of four identical, asymmetrical sections that are rotated around a center when they are assembled. Four of these sections make a 16" flower block. A 16" block is large enough so that it takes only twelve of them to make a full quilt if you are generous with your sashing and borders.

Because I do all my piecing with a sewing machine, these patterns are made with only straight seams.

When I see a timesaving or labor-saving hint, I usually try it at least once to see if it will work for me. I have stirred in a few of my "easy recipe" shortcuts that you may wish to try for yourself.

Origin of the Flower Designs

The first straight-edge flower design that I created was Day Lily. I began to make a quilt using only the Day Lily block with sashing when it occurred to me that the same technique I used in creating the Day Lily could be used to create other flower designs.

For a long time, I had wanted to make a blue-and-white quilt, so I made my original twelve flower blocks into a sampler quilt using dark blue-and-white prints on a white background. I was curious to see if the designs would still look flowerlike, even if they were made in most unflowerlike colors. You can judge for yourself by looking at the color photo of the quilt on page 17.

The Blue and White Sampler Quilt was my first attempt at making a flowered quilt with these patterns. Some, but not all, of the patterns for the flowers in that sampler quilt are given in this book. However, all the designs in the sampler use the templates in this book.

Create Your Own Floral Fantasies

Try these flowers for yourself. After you understand the grid and rotation system that I used to design them, you can create your own flower projects and even invent your own pieced flowers.

When I turned these designs and templates over to a few quilting friends to see how they would work, I found that I have very creative friends! They usually followed my block patterns, but the designs themselves inspired them to improvise in many directions, and the projects never turned out exactly as I had sent them out. Each took the opportunity to add her own individual touches to the settings and borders. I hope that all readers of this book will be inspired to do the same thing. Use this book as a starting point for creating your own floral fantasies.

Quilters need some phrase equivalent to Julia Child's *"Bon appetit!"* Perhaps *"Bon piquage!"* would be appropriate.

> **"**Use this book as a starting point for creating your own floral fantasies.**"**

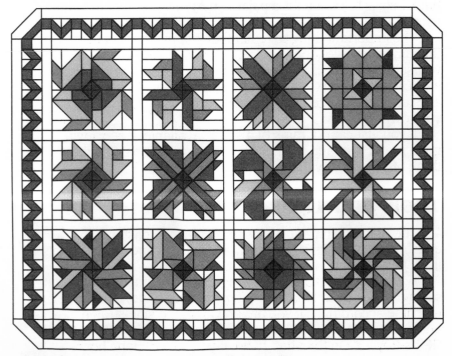

Fantasy Flowers, Blue & White Sampler Quilt, 68" x 86"

CONSTRUCTING FLOWERS AND OTHER FANTASIES

Every quilting project starts as an inspiration or fantasy in the mind of the quilter. The following material is meant to help you realize your own special quilted fantasies, whether with these flowered designs or any others.

Creating a Work Space

I hope that each of you has a special place for sewing, where you can keep your projects out and your sewing machine set up and available for working at odd moments. If you must clear off the dining room table every time you start and stop sewing, you need to look around your house more carefully for a sewing place of your own.

First, consider whose house this is. Those of you who have children and/or a husband know perfectly well that space is found for using and storing children's toys and husband's toys. Surely you can find room for your own toys!

• Most of you have no need for a guest room for fifty weeks of the year. If you are lucky enough to have a mostly unused room of any kind, turn it into a sewing room.

• If your family congregates around the television, is there a corner in that room for your sewing center?

• Finish off a corner of the basement or attic. Never mind decorating it; just be sure that you have enough heat and good lighting. Space is more important than carpet.

• Screen off a corner of your own bedroom.

• Put two of your children in the same bedroom and buy them bunk beds. (Tell them it's a pajama party!) Take over the other room for sewing.

The important thing to remember is that every member of the family deserves some space, and you should not shortchange yourself. Children should know that their parents have special interests that deserve respect and consideration. Don't live like a second-class citizen in your own home with no space to call your own.

If you just cannot think of a single available space, invite a good friend over and ask her to make suggestions. She may think of a possibility that you have overlooked.

> **66** *The important thing to remember is that every member of the family deserves some space, and you should not shortchange yourself.* **99**

Tools and Tips

The right equipment is essential for accomplishing any task efficiently. Take a lesson from smart workers and professionals in all fields, and treat yourself to the right tools.

• That you need a good sewing machine should go without saying. Know what kind of sewing you plan to do, and buy a machine accordingly. If you are only going to sew straight seams and hem up kitchen curtains occasionally, you do not need a "Rolls-Royce." On the other hand, if you spend many hours a week at the machine and if you want to do machine quilting, see that your machine is a good one. If the price of a good new machine bothers you, look at good second-hand machines. If the price bothers someone else in your family, consider the cost of outboard motors, power mowers, or golf clubs, for example. If you don't know how to clean your sewing machine and how to work with all its accessories, take a few lessons from your local dealer. Owning equipment that you are unable to use is pointless.

• Buy a good rotary cutter and a large cutting surface, and learn how to use them safely and well. These can be a real time-saver.

• Keep your edges sharp. Sharp knives work best in the kitchen, and sharp scissors are best in the sewing room. Buy a new blade for your rotary cutter as soon as you need one, not months later.

• Buy some good plastic rulers and cutting guides for rotary cutting. None of these things are for children's use, and they should be carefully put away when you are not using them. Rotary cutters are extremely sharp; keep them out of children's reach for their safety. Your good rulers and sharp scissors are too tempting to use for school projects; keep them out of sight so you can find them when you need them.

• If you are taller than average, as I am, consider putting your cutting table legs up on blocks to make a higher cutting surface. Bending over a table that is too low for a prolonged time can throw the most able back into a spasm.

• Have a large selection of "things to put things in." Among my favorites are the large plastic boxes in which the supermarket gets fish. Sometimes they will give them to you free; sometimes they will sell them to you for a small price. Or, cover sturdy cardboard boxes with self-adhesive paper so they will look pretty while holding your supplies. Use wire baskets or plastic dishpans to store your fabric.

• Put your containers on shelves. If you can't see your fabric, you will forget you have some of it. Sort it by color to make a beautiful rainbow effect for your sewing area. Use plastic bags or clear plastic shoe boxes for storing fabric scraps.

• The shelves can also be used to display and store your quilt books and magazines.

• Keep on hand a few cardboard fabric bolts from a fabric store. Pad one with batting, cover it with muslin, and use it as a portable ironing board. Cover another one with flannel or fleece and use it to hold the pieces of a block ready to be sewn on your sewing machine. You can even use them for their intended purpose and wrap long lengths of fabric on them.

• Keep your iron out and ready to use. The best place for it is where you can reach it from your sewing chair without having to stand up. Press seams as you go to keep things neat.

• Keep each project in a separate container along with all the fabric you are using for it. I use plastic dishpans for this.

• Throw away all the projects you know you will never finish. They are depressing to have around. If you can't bear to throw them out, give them to a friend or trade for her orphan projects. Get your quilt guild, church group, or club to have a UFO (Un-Finished Object) auction or swap night as a fund-raiser: you won't have made a discard, you will have made a donation.

Look hard at your present work space and your work habits. If you really want to spend time sewing, plan to make the most of your time by working neatly and efficiently.

"If you can't see your fabric, you will forget you have some of it."

"Throw away all the projects you know you will never finish. They are depressing to have around."

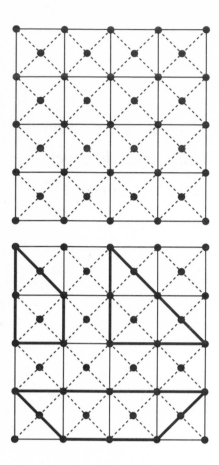

The Grid and the Templates

These flower patterns are constructed on a 2" grid, and most are on an 8"-square base, so each template can be used over and over for these designs and for other patterns based on a multiple of 2". The points on this grid make up the end points and corners on each of the template pieces.

Think of the construction as similar to the possible ways to put together the Tinker Toys you might have played with as a child. Every angle is either 45°, 90°, or 135°, because the grid lines go either straight or diagonally at the corners.

Each template piece follows a path along the possible lines of the grid. The illustration at left shows several templates superimposed on the grid.

Because these are standardized templates based on a 2" unit, I made myself a permanent set of templates that I can use for both traditional and new patterns, not just those in this book. See "Templates" section (page 63) for a discussion of how to make permanent templates.

Any of these flower patterns can be redrafted on a 1" grid to make smaller templates for finished flower blocks that are 8" square instead of 16". A set of smaller templates based on the 1" grid is included on pages 77–80.

Because all templates have been made on the 2" grid lines of an 8" block, nearly every piece can be changed or modified as shown with the T and Tr templates (at left). This allows you to change and modify any of the patterns while still using the templates given in this book. For instance, template J equals a combination of templates A and I. Among the triangles, B equals two As, and C equals two Bs. Templates D, E, F, and FF are just different lengths of a 2"-wide rectangle.

Some modifications that you could make might mean that some seams would not be straight. I purposely constrained myself to designing only with straight seams for this book.

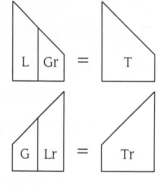

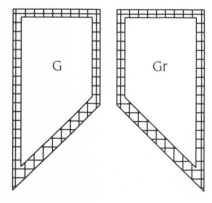

Using the Templates

Most of the templates given in this book are used in several of the flower blocks. The piecing diagrams give the template identification letters and show the placement of the pieces.

A ¼"-wide seam allowance is already marked on each template, and the seam allowance is printed with a grid pattern to indicate the preferred direction of the grain of the fabric when cutting. These templates are designed to make rotary cutting and machine quilting easy. If you are a dedicated hand-piecer, however, you can use the templates in your usual fashion. Some of the templates also have a mirror image of themselves. These are marked with a small letter "r" for reverse. G and Gr are mirror images of each other. When using the templates, it is important to cut all pieces from the same side of the fabric, because a G template cut on the reverse side of the fabric becomes a Gr when turned right side up.

Some of the templates need no mirror images because they are reversible as they are. Rectangles, triangles, and trapezoids are examples of this kind of template. With these, it does not matter whether the piece is cut from the right or wrong side of the fabric, and several layers of fabric may be cut at once.

If you cut all templates for a particular block on the reverse side of the fabric, you will make a reversed block that is the mirror image of the original drawing. I usually use both regular and reversed blocks when making a project with several of the same flowers in it, to add some variety to the design.

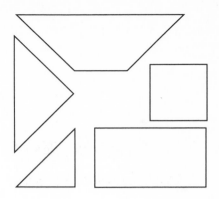

Creating the Designs

Most of the flower patterns are created by making the same asymmetrical 8" section four times and rotating them around a center axis in pinwheel fashion. If the templates are placed on the reverse side of the fabric for cutting, the reversed block will be a mirror image of the original.

The larger block shows four sections put together pinwheel fashion to make a flower block. The smaller illustration shows the same block when the templates are placed on the reverse side of the fabric.

Some of the flower patterns, such as Impatiens, Iris, Pansy, and Tall Tulip, do not rotate but, instead, use several mirror-image sections to create a flower block.

I assigned names to the flower blocks according to the flowers that they suggested to me, but the names are purely arbitrary. If my Red, Red Rose block looks like a peony to you, then it's a peony in your project. You can modify a block to make an original of your own, or you can use the grid and templates to design new and different flowers. Most of the templates you could possibly need are already in this book.

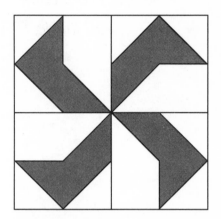

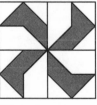

Mirror Image

Mixing Blocks and Settings

Because nearly all the flower blocks in this book are a standard 16" square, they can be used interchangeably in the settings and projects shown. If you prefer a different leaf pattern in your project, mix and match the leaf designs at the back of the book. Most of the leaf designs make up into 8" squares.

Before you piece the flower blocks for your quilt or wall-hanging project, decide on a suitable setting. A number of possible settings are shown in this book. Jot down a rough outline of your setting on graph paper and note the flower and leaf blocks that will be needed for your project. Feel free to substitute your own style of borders and bindings. It's your project!

Selecting the Fabrics

The assumption in this book is that you will be working with 44"-wide, 100% cotton fabrics. Wash and dry your fabric as soon as you buy it so it will be ready to use when inspiration strikes. Fold it flat for storage and stash it with other fabric in the same color group. Don't bother to press fabric until you are ready to use it—even then it may not be necessary.

"I set out piles of fabric in related colors as I work on a project so that I can 'paint' with fabric."

I usually prefer to cut my own bias strips from the fabric used in the project because it's better quality and wears better than commercially made bias tape. You may also use narrow ribbon for the flower stems.

Flower quilts that are made from many different fabrics provide variation in texture and design. Where several pieces in a block are to be cut of the same fabric, this is indicated by giving them the same "fill pattern" in the drawing and piecing diagram.

I find that I achieve a much more pleasant result if I select a background fabric and then cut each block individually, experimenting with combinations of color and size of fabric design as I go along. I set out piles of fabric in related colors as I work on a project so that I can "paint" with fabric. In making a project with three flower blocks, for instance, subtle color and texture variations in the blocks make the project more interesting. These are not exactly "scrap" projects in the usual sense, but I have certainly used a lot of my scraps in making them.

You may notice that many of the background fabrics used in this book are definitely not boring, off-white muslin! Splotchy-looking fabrics can make fine backgrounds when cut into small pieces. Experiment with new fabrics and become a bit more daring with each new project.

I seldom buy fabrics specifically for a given project. I buy fabrics that I really like when I see them, and eventually I select from among them for my projects. Yes, that means that I have accumulated a lot of fabric in my sewing room, but I consider this my working "palette." (If "she who dies with the most fabric wins," I am a definite contender!)

When deciding how much fabric to buy for a project, if there is any question in your mind, buy more rather than less! A whole project may be set aside and never finished if you were too stingy to buy enough fabric to finish it properly. You can spend months and years trying to find enough matching fabric to finish the project. Remember that leftovers are good! They are the basis for scrap quilts and the inspiration for new projects.

Cutting the Pieces

The templates (pages 63–80) are for use in all the flower blocks. Each is labeled with an identifying letter, and each has a ¼"-wide seam allowance added. The seam allowance on the template is printed in a grid pattern showing the correct grain line of the fabric. Be careful to cut according to the grain line for the best results.

Use your favorite method of tracing and reproducing the templates to suit your usual construction techniques.

Many of the templates are 2½" wide in one direction (2" plus two ¼" seam allowances). These may be economically cut from a 2½" strip of your fabric, one after the other, so that two of your template edges are already cut for you. Templates that may be cut this way are D, E, F, FF, G, Gr, H, Hr, I, Ir, K, L, Lr, LL, LLr, O, R, and Rr. This technique is not particularly useful when you are cutting

"When deciding how much fabric to buy for a project, if there is any question in your mind, buy more rather than less."

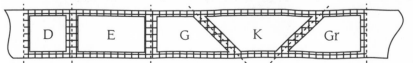

Dashed lines show cuts from 2½"-wide strip

your flower petals and mixing many fabrics because the pieces you need from a single fabric will be few, but it may be very helpful when you are cutting many pieces from the same fabric—for the background, for instance.

Working on a flannel board or a scrap of foam board insulation, I first lay out all the pieces for a block, arrange them on the board, and look them over to see whether I like the resulting blend of colors and textures before I start to sew. I take the board right to the sewing machine to keep the pieces in order, and I group them according to the piecing diagrams.

Never, never, never cut out all the pieces for a big project before you take a long look at several of the blocks after they are made up. You may decide to change the color scheme, and wouldn't you hate to have piles of cut pieces and nowhere to use them?

Assembling the Pieces

The piecing diagrams show how the pieces are assembled. This saves a lot of reading (like "Attach piece A to piece B before joining to piece F") and makes this book accessible to quilters who do not read English. Even without reading any directions, you can see how to assemble the fairly complicated Chrysanthemum block by looking at the piecing diagram.

First assemble the pieces that are shown attached to each other in the piecing diagrams, and then add the others as shown. If you ever come across something that is not a straight seam in these designs, you will know you have made a mistake in the order of the piecing. Look at the piecing diagram again.

Sewing Perfect Seams

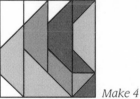

Make 4

When you cut pieces for any machine-pieced project, be very accurate. The seam lines are not marked on the fabric, so the accuracy of your cutting and the accuracy of your seam width are essential for the best results.

The ¼"-wide seam allowance is standard for quilting in the United States. However, templates with exact ¼"-wide seam allowances are only as good as you make them. Be sure that you can sew a perfectly accurate ¼"-wide seam before you begin a project.

Experiment by sewing straight edges together until your seams are exactly ¼". Some sewing machines have needles that adjust from side to side; try these adjustments. Try different presser feet to see which one has just the right edge to use as a guideline. Try marking the soleplate of your machine with a piece of masking tape at the right seam width. Keep experimenting until your seams are exactly right.

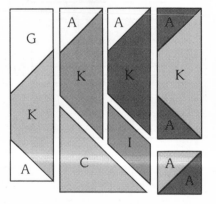

Sewing perfect seams will avoid all sorts of frustration as you try to put any quilting project together. Accuracy in cutting the fabric pieces and accuracy in sewing the seams will make every project fit together without marking the seam lines.

Most of these blocks can be done without pinning. As you work with these designs, you will notice that there are many places where seam lines do not have to be matched during construction. This makes for fast construction. Where seam lines must be

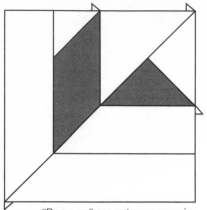

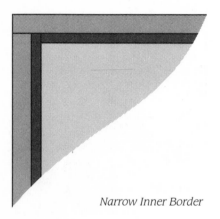

"Dog ears" are cuter on puppies

matched, you can pin before you sew, but you will be surprised at how few pins you will need on most of these projects.

I like to press seams as I work. Some quilters advise against this, but what they usually mean is "Don't stretch the raw edges," not "Don't press the seam." If you press seams carefully, without stretching the fabric, the next seams fit together better.

I also like to snip off the "dog ears" on the back of the project, but never until the block is finished. After I see that the block is correct, I snip away the ragged-looking "dog ears" that stick out beyond the seam allowances at the edge of the block. If you are making a project with many, many blocks, store them flat as they are completed to keep them neat.

Finishing

Planning Borders

Directions for some of the projects show borders and give measurements for them, and some simply suggest that you add borders if you wish. To decide on a proper border for your project, consider its eventual size and whether it will need to be set off from its background. A wall hanging with a light background that is meant to hang on a light-colored wall certainly needs a proper frame to set it off.

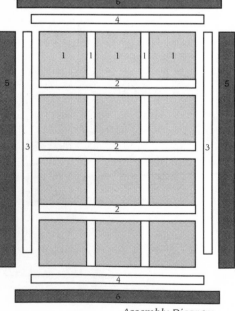

Narrow Inner Border

I prefer plain borders that are cut straight on the ends (rather than mitered) and added like the logs in a Log Cabin block. There are fewer ways to make a mistake with straight-cut borders, and you can add as many as you wish. Also, if your pieced center is not quite square, you can even it up by adding several rows of carefully measured borders. If you prefer borders with mitered corners, they should be carefully finished so that the piece is square.

A narrow inner border in a dark or bright contrasting color is sometimes just the thing needed to set off a design. If borders are cut 1" wide, they finish to ½". This is a good width to introduce just a bit of spice to the project.

Two pieced borders, Scalloped Border (page 58) and Leafy Border (page 49), are included in this book. Many of the leaf blocks can be used in border designs as well.

Assembling Your Project

Many of these flower blocks have designs that extend right to the edge of the block. For that reason, they often look best when separated by leaf blocks or sashing. Examples of combining flower blocks and leaf blocks are shown in many of the projects.

The borders shown in this book are made of simple strips sewn on with straight seams. The assembly diagram below shows an efficient way to put together a simple setting of twelve quilt blocks with sashing and borders. The sashing is represented by the white strips. Assemble in this order:

Assembly Diagram

1. Quilt blocks and interior vertical sashing in horizontal rows
2. Interior horizontal sashing added to rows of blocks
3. Outer vertical sashing strips
4. Outer horizontal sashing strips
5. Outer vertical border strips
6. Outer horizontal border strips

Making the Quilt Back

Some quilters are making the backs of their quilts so interesting these days that I am expecting to see a whole book on quilt backs soon. However, I will assume that you want a plain back on your quilt. After all, we are trying to get this project done!

You will almost certainly have at least one seam on the back of a quilt, and you may need to seam together the back for a large wall hanging. Plan these seams so that they do not occur in the same place as major seams on the front, because the resulting bulk would make quilting more difficult.

When deciding how to put together the quilt back, remember that the backing and batting should be several inches larger all around than the quilt top. Cut the selvage edges off the fabric before you sew any seams so that the backing will "give" if necessary; selvage edges are too rigid to be used in quilting.

At right are several possible ways to seam together quilt backs. As you plan your seams for the backing, consider using several different fabrics—maybe even the leftovers from your project—and you will be well on your way to creating an attractive quilt back.

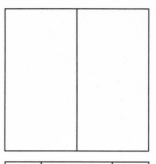
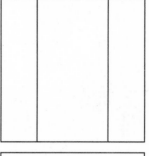

Quilt Backs

Choosing the Batting

The batting you choose should be appropriate for the project and easy to use, and it shouldn't make you unhappy. Thin batting is easier to quilt through than thick batting. Medium batting is OK for machine quilting, but really thick batting is suitable only for tied quilts.

Some hand quilters swear by cotton batting and others by wool, but most of us use the more readily available synthetic battings.

I sometimes use lightweight polyester fleece (sold by the yard from a bolt) for wall hangings. I like the fleece for this purpose because it is firm and flat, and I find it easy to square up a wall hanging on it.

If you are a beginner, get recommendations and advice on batting from your friends who quilt. Try out a few kinds, then settle on something that you find easy to handle.

Basting—aarrgh!

Ironing is the chore I hate most, but next to that I dislike having to sew by hand. Even worse is basting quilts—a chore inevitably done on your knees or bent over in some other uncomfortable position. If it is absolutely essential for your mental health that your quilt top be basted, invite some quilting friends over, bribe them with a good lunch or dessert, and have them help you get it done. (Promise them "quilt sandwiches"—sorry!)

If your mental health can stand the thought of an unbasted quilt sandwich, buy several hundred safety pins about 1¼" long. (Use really good safety pins that don't have rough points and don't use thick pins.) Spread out your quilt back on the floor with the right side down, or attach it with masking tape to a Ping-Pong table top if you are lucky enough to have one.

Carefully place the batting on top of the backing to avoid stretching the batting. Spread the quilt top on the batting, getting it as square as possible. Then, start at one end and pin your way to the other end, spacing safety pins every 6" and smoothing the quilt top as you work. Pin through the entire quilt sandwich and fasten the pins securely.

When you are about one-fourth done with the pinning, turn the pinned part over carefully and see whether everything is flat. If not, take out the offending pins and try again. Once you get the hang of it, the pinning goes very quickly, and you can hum a little tune dedicated to all that tedious basting that you are not doing.

Quilting Designs

As a general rule, curved quilting designs soften straight lines, and I recommend them for these flower blocks. One of my favorites is a sort of free-form petal on top of the flower petals in the blocks. These can be done either by hand or by machine and need not be drawn on the block. Just start stitching.

Because the designs are on a 2" grid, quilting along the grid lines is an easy way to do the quilting, but you can see in the illustration how much better the curves look. You might want to try a combination of effects by doing curved quilting on the flowers and a grid design on the background as in the Blue and White Sampler (page 17). The grid tends to make the seams disappear on the background pieces.

I no longer mark quilt patterns on blocks, except occasionally with narrow masking tape or a little chalk. I don't like the problem of removing markings from the fabric. It can be done, but it is often not done properly or thoroughly.

Some quilters cut shapes from self-adhesive paper and use them as templates to quilt around. One quilter claims she draws random curved lines on the back of a quilt and then quilts from the back! She is an excellent quilter, and her stitches look good on the front, but I know mine never would.

Quilting

As my husband frequently says in answer to nearly any question at all, "There are probably several very excellent books on the subject." Many books have been written about hand quilting and quilting stitches. Read some of them!

Read about machine quilting too. If your sewing machine does not have a walking foot, buy one and start practicing. Try hand-guided, free-style machine quilting with your feed dog down and using your darning foot. Like getting to Carnegie Hall, it takes practice, practice, practice.

Crib quilts should definitely be machine quilted. Only doting, first-time grandmothers make hand-quilted crib quilts. (Crib quilts get all sorts of yucky stuff on them and must be washed frequently, which is very hard on delicate hand quilting.)

Trimming the Quilt

When all the quilting is done, carefully trim off the ragged edges of the backing and batting. Be very careful to protect the edge of the quilt top with a heavy plastic ruler while using your rotary cutter. Make sure that the corners are square and the edges are matching lengths. Now is the time to trim off an extra ⅛" if the sides are slightly different lengths.

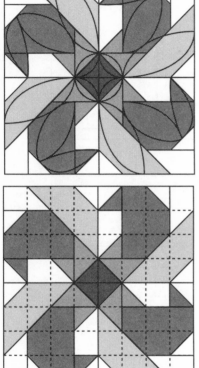

The curved design appears much more flowerlike than the grid design

"Machine quilting, like getting to Carnegie Hall, takes practice, practice, practice."

Making a Sleeve for a Wall Hanging

Before you bind the project is the time to decide whether or not you want to add a sleeve for hanging it on a wall. If you do, cut a 6½"-wide strip of fabric the width of your wall hanging. A narrower sleeve is fine, but some quilt shows ask to have a 5"–6" sleeve, so a wider one will meet all circumstances.

Hem both ends of the sleeve so that the length is about 1" in from each side of the quilt. Hem the bottom edge of the sleeve with the sewing machine. Pin the top raw edge to the back of the top of the quilt. When you machine stitch the binding, the sleeve will be attached firmly to the quilt. Pin the bottom edge in place and blindstitch it to the back of the quilt.

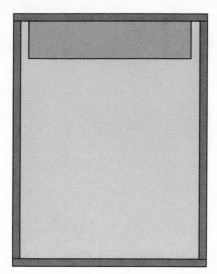

I use a narrow piece of ¼"-thick wooden lattice about 1½" wide to hang wall hangings with sleeves. Cut the board about 1" shorter than the width of the wall hanging. Sand the board lightly to remove splinters. Drill a ¼" hole about ½" in from each end. Use the holes in the board to mark where nails go on the wall; put small nails in the wall to hang the board; insert board in sleeve, and hang. The small, thin board keeps the wall hanging close to the wall, and small nails keep holes to a minimum.

Write the name of the wall hanging on the board for easy identification.

| ○ | QUILT NAME | ○ |

Binding

Nowhere is it written in stone that bindings must be cut on the bias. For quilts with curved or scalloped edges, bias binding does work best. But for all straight-edged projects, the binding is firmer, less likely to stretch, and easier to work with if it is cut on the straight grain of the fabric.

Bindings don't have to be dull, plain colors. They can be made from prints, stripes, and plaids. They can be pieced from many different scraps used in the project. Think about the effect you want on your quilt.

I like quilt bindings made double because the binding is where a quilt wears out first. I recommend double binding for wall hangings, too, because it makes a firmer edge.

For double-layer binding, cut fabric strips six times the width you want the finished binding to be, plus ¼" to ½". (That "plus" fabric disappears into the thickness of your batting.) For example, to make a binding that finishes to ¼" wide, cut a strip 1¾" to 2" wide. A ½"-wide finished double binding is made with 3½"-wide strips.

Quilt judges used to absolutely love tiny, narrow bindings stuffed so full that they were stiff, but how much do you hang around with quilt judges? If you prefer a wider binding, make it the way you want it.

Cut the ends of the binding strips at a 45° angle and piece as shown on page 16. This diagonal seam makes less of a lump when it is doubled.

Fold the binding strip in half lengthwise, wrong sides together, with raw edges even. Press.

> **❝**Nowhere is it written in stone that bindings must be cut on the bias.**❞**

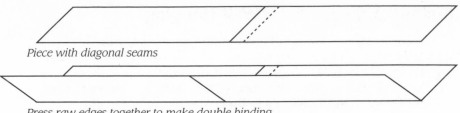

Piece with diagonal seams

Press raw edges together to make double binding

Using the walking foot on your sewing machine, stitch the raw edges of the binding to the raw edge of the right side of the quilt.

Leaving a 6" length of binding strip hanging free, start sewing in the middle of one side. Check your binding strip to make sure that a piecing seam does not fall at a corner, making it hard to turn a neat corner. Stitch ¼" from the edge of the quilt; backstitch and cut the threads.

Turn the quilt and fold the binding flat and even with the just-stitched edge as shown in the illustration at left. Start stitching ¼" from the end, backstitching a bit to lock the stitches. Stitch to the next corner and repeat.

When you have gone all the way around the quilt except for the last 12", stop sewing and trim the ends of your binding strips with diagonal edges, carefully measuring to allow them to be seamed together. (Cut them a little longer than you think necessary; it's always easier to trim them down if they are too long.) Sew the ends together and check for fit. Then, finish sewing the binding to the quilt.

When the binding is folded over to the back, the corners can be folded the same way so that you have a mitered corner on the back. Hand stitch the folded edge of the binding to the back of the quilt to just cover the machine-stitching line.

If you make a binding wider than ¼", you may need some extra stuffing to make a really firm edge. If so, you can insert narrow strips of batting as "falsies" as you hand stitch the back of the binding in place.

Autograph Time

Quilt historians are making us more and more aware of the loss to our historical knowledge that has resulted from the fact that, in the past, most women did not sign and date their quilts. No matter how big or small your project, put your name on it, with the year it was made and the town and state where you live.

If you press freezer paper to the back of a piece of light-colored fabric, it will make the fabric stiff enough to write on with an indelible ink pen. (Be sure it is permanent ink–wash a sample of the writing before you attach it to your quilt, no matter what some clerk told you!) You can even run the fabric/paper through a typewriter and type the information on your label. Do a test piece first to be sure the typewritten ink won't rub off or run in the wash.

Remove the freezer paper. Turn under the raw edges of the quilt label and attach to the lower right-hand side of the quilt back.

Happy quilting! Bon piquage!

❝*No matter how big or small your project, put your name on it.***❞**

GALLERY

Blue and White Sampler with Scalloped Border
    Doreen C. Burbank, 1990, Windham, New Hampshire, 68"x 86". The first project made with these flower designs was this Blue and White Sampler quilt, which was juried into the New England Images III show; machine pieced and machine quilted by the author.

Flower Garden Sampler

Doreen C. Burbank, 1991, Windham, New Hampshire, 42" x 57". This sampler wall hanging made with the small templates uses all the flower designs in this book and most of the leaf designs; machine pieced and machine quilted by the author.

Daffodils in the Rain

Karen E. Senet, 1991, Londonderry, New Hampshire, 29" x 57". Done in pastels, this wall hanging features separate sections of the Daffodil design; machine pieced and machine quilted.

Jinny's Night-bines

Joan Emery Ross, 1991, Andover, Massachusetts, 41" x 32". Joan made this wall hanging using the small templates, a Jinny Beyer fabric sampler, and the Columbine design; machine pieced and hand quilted.

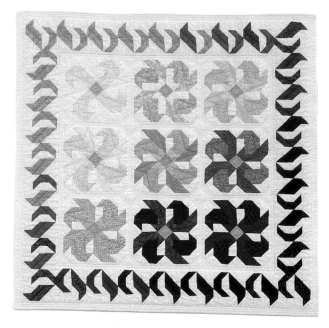

My Mother's Garden

Joan Emery Ross, 1991, Andover, Massachusetts, 38" x 38". Using the small templates and the Day Lily design, Joan made this wall hanging for her mother, who has a garden full of day lilies; machine pieced and hand quilted.

De-Vine Inspiration

Carol A. Babineau, 1991, Windham, New Hampshire, 75" x 92". Featuring the Bunch of Daisies design in primary colors, this full-size quilt is machine pieced and machine quilted in a vinelike design. Carol machine quilted a "poison ivy" design around the border, "so nobody touches my quilt!"

Impatiens

Roxanne Carter, 1992, Mukilteo, Washington, 28" x 56". Roxanne's Impatiens are softly colored in shades of pink set off by complementary green leaves on a crisp white ground. Machine pieced and machine quilted.

Impatiens

Karen E. Senet, 1991, Londonderry, New Hampshire, 28" x 56". Karen's bright Impatiens float on a boldly colored background. Machine pieced and machine quilted.

Karen's Iris

Karen E. Senet, 1991, Londonderry, New Hampshire, 80" x 62". Karen, who is a member of the American Iris Society, modified the original Iris design and created the Bud and Leaf block for this large wall hanging; machine pieced and machine quilted.

Purple Pansy Patch

Nancy J. Martin, 1992, Woodinville, Washington, 31½" x 20". Perky purple pansies on a soft pink background are surrounded by a striped border. Hand quilted by Nancy Sweeney.

Pansy Patch

Karla Kamens Cook, 1991, Andover, Massachusetts, 57" x 78". Karla, who makes many crib quilts for young relatives, used the Pansy design to create this crib quilt. The machine quilting includes two butterflies and a lady bug; machine pieced and machine quilted.

Red, Red Rose

Doreen C. Burbank, 1991, Windham, New Hampshire, 46" x 46". This wall hanging features the Red, Red Rose design with a thorny border; machine pieced by the author and beautifully machine quilted by Carol Babineau.

Poinsettias

Doreen C. Burbank, 1989, Windham, New Hampshire, 24" x 60". The Burbanks' inside back door "dresses up" in this Poinsettia wall hanging during the Christmas season; machine pieced and machine quilted.

Field of Sunflowers

Doreen C. Burbank, 1991, Windham, New Hampshire, 39" x 63". The fields of Kansas, the author's native state, were the inspiration for the design and bright colors of this wall hanging featuring the Sunflower design. Three different background fabrics were used; machine pieced and machine quilted.

FLOWER DESIGNS

Bachelor Buttons

Bachelor Buttons is an airy design that uses the very simplest of templates. I like it with the flower pieces made from different scraps of pale to medium blue with yellow centers and assorted green scraps used for leaves in the wall hanging. This flower block would also be very attractive in the setting used for the Bunch of Daisies quilt.

To make one finished 16"-square Bachelor Buttons block, follow the cutting and block assembly directions below.

Cutting

Use templates A, B, C, E, and Gr.

✂ From background fabric, cut 8 of template E and 4 each of templates B, C, and Gr.

✂ From assorted blue fabrics, cut 12 of template B and 4 each of templates C and E.

✂ From yellow fabric, cut 4 of template A for center piece.

Block Assembly

1. Make four 8"-square Bachelor Buttons sections, following the piecing diagram.
2. Assemble block, rotating each section one-quarter turn around the A center pieces.

Note: Make the reversed block shown in the wall hanging by cutting the same templates from the wrong side of the fabric.

Bachelor Buttons and Leaves Wall Hanging
24" x 48"

Materials

44"-wide fabric

1 yd. background fabric
½ yd. assorted blue fabrics for flower petals
⅛ yd. yellow fabric for flower centers
¼ yd. green fabric for leaves
1 yd. bias strip or narrow ribbon, ¼"–½" wide, for stems
½ yd. for binding
1½ yds. for backing
Batting and thread to finish

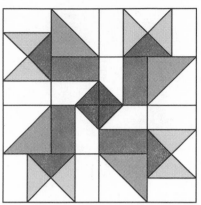

16" Bachelor Buttons Block

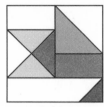

8" Bachelor Buttons Section

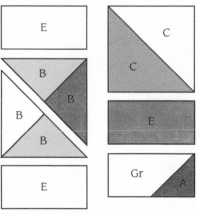

Piecing Diagram

Directions

1. Following the diagrams, cut and piece:
   1 Bachelor Buttons block
   1 reversed Bachelor Buttons block
   6 Leaf #1 blocks (page 59)
   3 Leaf #3 blocks (page 59)
2. Cut one 8½" x 8½" square of background fabric.
3. Assemble blocks and background square into wall-hanging top, following diagram.
4. Layer wall-hanging top with batting and backing. Quilt and bind as desired.

Bachelor Buttons and Leaves Wall Hanging

Chrysanthemum

In contrast to the airy Bachelor Buttons block, Chrysanthemum is a very solid-looking flower with little background fabric in the block. The colors should be carefully planned, as it is important that the four petals in each 8" section be well defined. Note that three of them involve several pieces. I chose to order the petals medium light, medium, medium dark, medium to provide subtle contrast and definition.

To make one finished 16"-square Chrysanthemum block, follow the cutting and block assembly directions below.

Cutting

Use templates A, C, G, I, and K.

✂ From the medium light fabric, cut 4 each of templates C and K.

✂ From one medium fabric, cut 4 each of templates A, I, and K.

✂ From the other medium fabric, cut 4 of template K.

✂ From the medium dark fabric, cut 8 of template A and 4 of template K.

✂ From the flower-center fabric, cut 4 of template A.

✂ From the background fabric, cut 12 of template A and 4 of template G.

Block Assembly

1. Make four 8"-square Chrysanthemum sections, following the piecing diagram.
2. Assemble block, rotating each section one-quarter turn around the A center pieces.

Note: Make the reversed block as shown in the quilt plan by cutting the same templates from the wrong side of the fabric.

Chrysanthemums and Flying Leaves Wall Hanging

44" x 44", plus borders

The name of this wall hanging suggests that fall has come and leaves are flying, so fall colors are appropriate for the leafy blocks that surround the flower blocks. Leaf #8 is a variation of the Flying Geese pattern. The placement of the leaf blocks appears to be random, but if you put your wall hanging together exactly as I did, you will see that the direction of each block was carefully planned.

16" Chrysanthemum Block

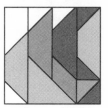

8" Chrysanthemum Section

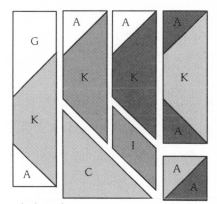

Piecing Diagram

Materials

44"-wide fabric

1 yd. background fabric
½ yd. each of 4 fabrics for flower petals—
    1 medium dark, 2 medium, 1 medium light
⅛ yd. for flower centers
1 yd. assorted green fabrics or fall colors for flying leaves
Border fabrics as desired
2¾ yds. for backing
½ yd. for binding
Batting and thread to finish

Directions

1. Following the diagrams, cut and piece:
   2 Chrysanthemum blocks
   2 reversed Chrysanthemum blocks
   57 Leaf #8 blocks (page 60)
2. Assemble blocks into wall-hanging top, following diagram.
3. Add borders as desired. (See page 12.)
4. Layer wall-hanging top with batting and backing. Quilt and bind as desired.

Chrysanthemum and Flying Leaves Wall Hanging

Columbine

Columbine is an angular design, pictured as one flower blossom facing you. The natural colors of the columbine offer a wide range of possibilities, from very delicate to extremely vivid. I have designed this with several matching fabrics in each section to define the center of the flower and the outer petals. Another choice of color placement could result in a very different-looking flower.

To make one finished 16"-square Columbine block, follow the cutting and block assembly directions below.

Cutting

Use templates A, B, BB, CC, and Gr.

✂ From background fabric, cut 4 each of templates B and CC, and 8 of template Gr.

✂ From petal fabric #1, cut 4 of template BB.

✂ From petal fabric #2, cut 4 each of templates B and A.

✂ From petal fabric #3, cut 4 each of templates B and A.

✂ From flower-center fabric, cut 4 of template A.

Block Assembly

1. Make four 8"-square Columbine sections, following the piecing diagram.
2. Assemble block, rotating each section one-quarter turn around the A center pieces.

Columbine Wall Hanging

57" x 33"

Materials

44"-wide fabric

1 yd. background fabric
¼ yd. each of 3 different fabrics for flower petals
⅛ yd. fabric for flower centers
¼ yd. for leaves
¼ yd. for inner border (Strips will need to be pieced.)
1¾ yds. for outer border and binding
½ yd. bias strip or ribbon, ¼"–½" wide, for stems
1¾ yds. for backing
Batting and thread to finish

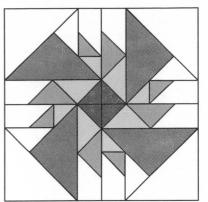

16" Columbine Block

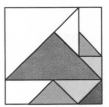

8" Columbine Section

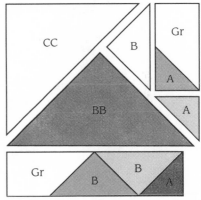

Piecing Diagram

Directions

1. Following the diagrams, cut and piece:
   3 Columbine blocks
   4 Leaf #1 blocks (page 59)
   1 Leaf #3 block (page 59)
2. Cut one 8½" x 8½" square of background fabric.
3. Assemble blocks into center section, following diagram.
4. For the inner border, cut 2 strips, 1" x 48½", and cut 2 strips, 1" x 25½".
5. For the outer border, cut 2 strips, 4½" x 25½", and 2 strips, 4½" x 57½".
6. Assemble wall hanging by adding the top and bottom inner border to the center section; add the side strips of the inner and outer border; finish by adding the top and bottom outer border strips. (See assembly diagram.)
7. Layer wall-hanging top with batting and backing. Quilt and bind as desired.

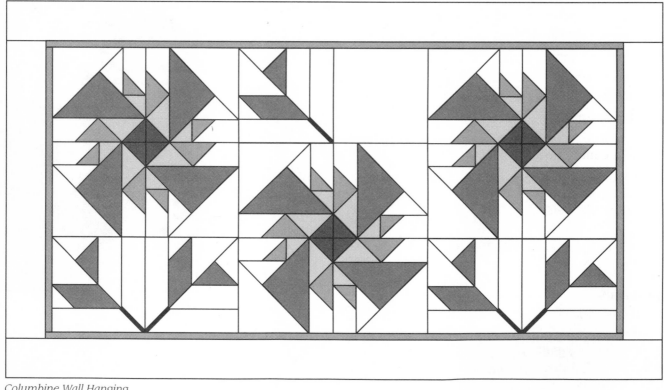

Columbine Wall Hanging

Daffodil

If the Daffodil design is made into a 16" block, it appears as four blossoms on a single stalk. However, in the Daffodils in the Rain wall hanging, the separate 8" sections are arranged vertically on stems. The diagonal dashed lines on the drawing illustrate one way of quilting the wall hanging so that the flowers appear to be in a spring rain.

To make one finished 16"-square Daffodil block, follow the cutting and block assembly directions below.

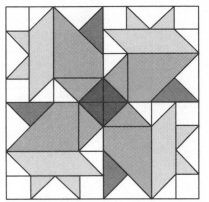

16" Daffodil Block

Cutting

Use templates A, B, D, Rr, and T.

- ✂ From background fabric, cut 12 of template A, 8 of template B, and 8 of template D.
- ✂ From light yellow fabric, cut 4 of template Rr and 8 of template A.
- ✂ From medium yellow fabric, cut 4 each of templates B and T.
- ✂ From dark yellow fabric, cut 4 of template B.
- ✂ From light green fabric, cut 4 of template A.

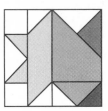

8" Daffodil Section

Block Assembly

1. Make 4 Daffodil sections, following the piecing diagram.
2. Assemble block, rotating each section one-quarter turn around the A center pieces.

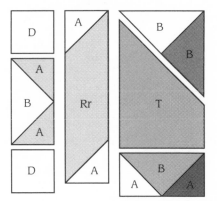

Piecing Diagram

Daffodils in the Rain Wall Hanging
24" x 52", plus borders

The easiest way to construct the Daffodils in the Rain wall hanging is in vertical rows. This means that the right and left halves of the Daffodil sections are not sewn together until the piece is assembled. Cut the pieces of the reversed flower sections by following the reversed piecing diagram given and using the templates indicated. Bias strips or ribbon stems are appliquéd over the seam lines after the top is assembled.

Note: Make the reversed block sections used in the wall hanging by following the piecing diagram and instructions on the next page. Use templates A, B, D, R, and Tr for reversed sections.

Materials
44"-wide fabric

1½ yds. background fabric
½ yd. light yellow fabric for flower petals
½ yd. medium yellow fabric for flower petals
¼ yd. dark yellow fabric for flower petals
½ yd. light green fabric for leaves and flower centers
2¼ yds. bias strip or ribbon, ¼"–½" wide, for stems
Border fabrics as desired
1¾ yds. for backing
Binding, batting, and thread to finish

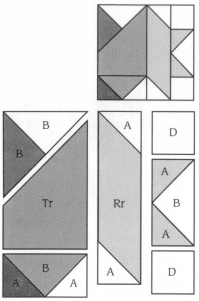

*Piecing Diagram for Reversed
Daffodil Sections*

Directions

1. Following the diagrams, cut and piece:
   2 Daffodil 8" sections (with left and right halves of sections unattached)
   3 reversed Daffodil 8" sections (with left and right halves of sections unattached)
   12 Leaf #5 blocks (page 60)
   2 Leaf #6 blocks (page 60)
   4 Leaf #7 blocks (page 60)
2. From the background fabric, cut:
   1 strip, 4½" x 24½", for the left side
   1 strip, 4½" x 16½", for the right side
   3 strips, 4½" x 12½", for the top
   15 squares, 4½" x 4½"
3. Assemble the wall hanging in vertical rows as shown in the assembly diagram.
4. Add borders as desired. (See page 12.)
5. Appliqué bias strip or ribbon over piecing seams for stems.
6. Layer wall-hanging top with batting and backing. Quilt and bind as desired.

Daffodils in the Rain Wall Hanging

32

Daisy

The Daisy design looks rather thin and lonely when displayed singly—as does the flower itself when alone. But when daisies are gathered into a bunch, they make a lovely display.

To make one finished 16"-square Daisy block, follow the cutting and block assembly directions below.

Cutting

Use templates A, C, K, M, and O.

- ✂ From the background fabric, cut 8 of template C, 4 of template K, and 12 of template A.
- ✂ From petal fabric #1, cut 4 of template O.
- ✂ From petal fabric #2, cut 4 of template M.
- ✂ From petal fabric #3, cut 4 of template K and 8 of template A.
- ✂ From flower-center fabric, cut 4 of template A.

Block Assembly

1. Make four 8"-square Daisy sections, following the piecing diagram.
2. Assemble block, rotating each section one-quarter turn around the A center pieces.

Bunch of Daisies Quilt

72" x 96"

The Bunch of Daisies quilt was originally conceived as white daisies with yellow centers on a pastel background. When one of my quilting friends, Carol Babineau, actually began to work with the design, she decided on primary colors for her quilt top and made a Painted Daisy quilt. She said that it was the first quilt (of many, many beautiful ones she has made) that her daughter, Sarah, asked to have for her own.

Materials

44"-wide fabric

6 yds. background fabric
½ yd. each of 3 different fabrics for flower petals
¼ yd. fabric for flower centers
¾ yd. fabric for leaves
3 yds. bias strip or ribbon, ¼"–½" wide, for stems
1 yd. for binding
6 yds. for backing
Batting and thread to finish

16" Daisy Block

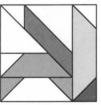

8" Daisy Section

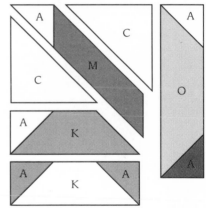

Piecing Diagram

Directions

1. From background fabric, cut:
   2 strips, 4½" x 96½", for side borders
   2 strips, 8½" x 64½", for top and bottom borders
   12 pieces, 8½" square
   8 pieces, 4½" x 8½"
2. Following the diagrams, cut and piece:
   8 Daisy blocks
   4 Daisy 8"-square sections
   8 Leaf #1 blocks (page 59)
   12 Leaf #2 blocks (page 59)
   6 Leaf #3 blocks (page 59)
   2 Leaf #4 blocks (page 59)
3. Assemble blocks into quilt top, following assembly diagram.
4. Add top and bottom borders; add side borders.
5. Layer quilt top with batting and backing. Quilt and bind as desired.

Bunch of Daisies Quilt

Day Lily

Day Lily was the first of this series of flower blocks that I designed, and it remains one of my favorites—among my quilt designs and as a flower that makes a dramatic summer accent in my backyard.

If the A and B templates that surround the center pieces are cut of the same fabric, they create a star pattern that you may or may not want to have stand out in your block. Be careful that this star does not contrast too much with the other fabrics, or it will be the focal point instead of the flower shape.

Note that template U and one of the A templates are cut from the same fabric to create a curved petal.

To make one finished 16"-square Day Lily block, follow the cutting and block assembly directions below.

16" Day Lily Block

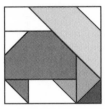

8" Day Lily Section

Cutting

Use templates A, B, G, Q, and U.

- ✂ From the background fabric, cut 12 of template A and 8 of template G.
- ✂ From petal fabric #1, cut 4 of template Q.
- ✂ From petal fabric #2, cut 4 each of templates A and U.
- ✂ From petal fabric #3, cut 4 each of templates A and B.
- ✂ From flower-center fabric, cut 4 of template A.

Block Assembly

1. Make 4 Day Lily sections, following piecing diagram.
2. Assemble block, rotating each section one-quarter turn around the A center pieces.

Note: Make the reversed block shown in the wall hanging by cutting the same templates from the wrong side of the fabric.

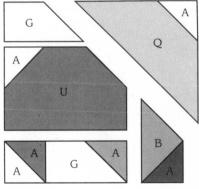

Piecing Diagram

Day Lily Wall Hanging

20" x 56"

The first examples that I made of the Day Lily were in the unlikely shades of blue and white. However, day lilies come in a startling array of colors in nature and can be portrayed in any color scheme.

Materials

44"-wide fabric

1½ yds. background fabric
¼ yd. each of 3 different fabrics for flower petals
⅛ yd. fabric for flower centers
½ yd. for binding
1¾ yds. for backing
Batting and thread to finish

Directions

1. From background fabric, cut:
   2 strips, 2½" x 52½", for side borders
   2 strips, 2½" x 20½", for top and bottom borders
   2 sashing strips, 2½" x 16½"
2. Following the diagram, cut and piece:
   2 Day Lily blocks
   1 reversed Day Lily block
3. Assemble wall-hanging top with sashing between pieced blocks as shown in the diagram. Add side borders. Add top and bottom borders.
4. Layer wall-hanging top with batting and backing. Quilt and bind as desired.

Day Lily Wall Hanging

Impatiens

The Impatiens block is made from four different 8"-square sections, and the right and left sides are mirror images of each other. Piecing diagrams are provided for all four sections.

Brightly colored impatiens in shades of red, pink, or white contrast sharply with the darker leaves that ring this block. (If you make white impatiens, be sure they contrast with the background fabric and use several shades of near-white to define the individual petals of the flower.)

These blocks include their own small leaf parts. When used in a project and combined with graceful leaf blocks that blend into them, the flowers appear to float above a background of tiny leaves. To make leaves, try to buy several kinds of green fabric that look almost the same from a distance but will provide a bit of texture and contrast when viewed close up.

Use the same closely-related-but-slightly-different approach when selecting fabrics for the flower in this block. Choose two shades of a color for all of the flowers in your project, or make each block different by selecting petal fabrics from a larger assortment of colors.

To make one finished 16"-square Impatiens block, follow the cutting and block assembly directions below.

Cutting

For the upper left and right sections, use templates A, B, C, G, Gr, J, and U.

- ✂ From the background fabric, cut 6 of template A and 2 each of templates B and C.
- ✂ From green fabric, cut 2 each of templates B and J.
- ✂ From petal fabric #1, cut 2 each of templates A, G, and Gr.
- ✂ From petal fabric #2, cut 2 of template U.
- ✂ From flower-center fabric, cut 2 of template A.

For the lower left and right sections, use templates A, B, G, Gr, J, K, and U.

- ✂ From the background fabric, cut 10 of template A, 2 of template B, and 1 each of templates G and Gr.
- ✂ From green fabric, cut 2 each of templates B and J.
- ✂ From petal fabric #1, cut 2 each of templates K and U.
- ✂ From petal fabric #2, cut 2 of template B.
- ✂ From flower-center fabric, cut 2 of template A.

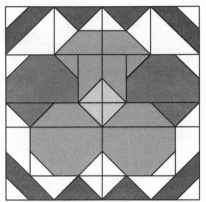

16" Impatiens Block

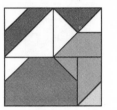

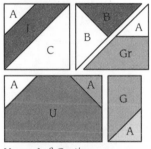

Upper Left Section

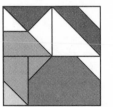

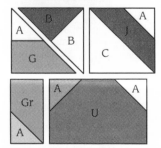

Upper Right Section

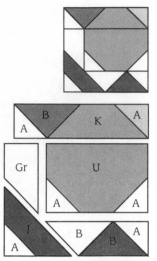

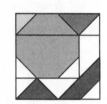

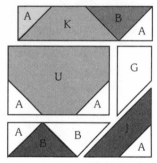

Lower Left Section

Lower Right Section

Block Assembly

1. Make the 4 different 8" sections, following the piecing diagrams.
2. Assemble the block.

Impatiens Wall Hanging

28" x 56"

This project requires three completed Impatiens blocks that are either identical in color or slightly different. Keep color variation to a minimum in Impatiens projects as it is already a very busy design. The top and bottom pieced borders of the wall hanging are made of A and B triangles that continue the leafy theme.

Materials

44"-wide fabric

1¼ yds. background fabric
1½ yds. assorted green fabric for borders and leaves
   (closely related in color and design)
¼ yd. each of 2 different fabrics for flower petals
⅛ yd. fabric for flower centers
1¾ yds. for backing
½ yd. for binding
Batting and thread to finish

Directions

1. From green, cut:
   2 strips, 2½" x 52½", for side borders
   2 strips, 2½" x 28½", for top and bottom solid borders
2. Following the diagrams, cut and piece:
   3 Impatiens blocks
   6 Leaf #11 blocks (page 61)
3. For top and bottom pieced borders, cut:
   4 of template A and 10 of template B from green
   12 of template B from background fabric
4. Assemble the pieced borders, following diagram below.
5. Assemble pieced blocks and top and bottom pieced borders into wall-hanging top, following assembly diagram. Add side borders, then top and bottom solid borders.
6. Layer wall-hanging top with batting and backing. Quilt and bind as desired.

Pieced Top and Bottom Border Strip for Impatiens Wall Hanging

Impatiens Quilt

76" x 88"

The Impatiens quilt is a larger version of the wall hanging and uses the same elements. Assemble pieced blocks into three vertical or five horizontal sections, then join the sections into the quilt top. The top and bottom pieced borders are larger versions of the one shown for the wall hanging.

Materials

44"-wide fabric

4 yds. total of assorted green fabrics for leaves, borders, and binding
1¼ yds. each of 2 different fabrics for flower petals
¼ yd. fabric for flower centers
3 yds. background fabric
5¾ yds. for backing
Batting and thread to finish

Directions

1. From green, cut:
   2 strips, 2½" x 80½", for side borders
   2 strips, 2½" x 76½", for top and bottom solid borders
2. Following the diagrams, cut and piece:
   15 Impatiens blocks
   30 Leaf #11 blocks (page 61)
3. From the green, cut 4 of template A and 34 of template B. From the background fabric, cut 36 of template B. Assemble top and bottom pieced borders, referring to the quilt diagram.
4. Assemble completed blocks and top and bottom pieced borders into quilt top, referring to assembly diagram. Add side borders. Add top and bottom solid borders.
5. Layer quilt top with batting and backing. Quilt and bind as desired.

Impatiens Wall Hanging

Impatiens Quilt

Iris

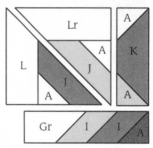

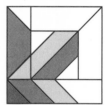

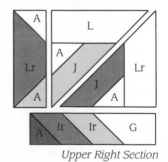

16" Iris Block

Upper Left Section

Upper Right Section

The iris is a showy flower and can make a showy project. The tall leaves used with it are representative of the spiky leaves of the iris plant. The Iris block is made from four different 8" sections. Piecing diagrams are given for each section.

To make one finished 16"-square Iris block, follow the cutting and block assembly directions below.

Cutting

For the upper left and right sections, use templates A, G, Gr, I, Ir, J, K, L, and Lr.

- ✂ From the background fabric, cut 6 of template A, 2 each of templates L and Lr, and 1 each of templates G and Gr.
- ✂ From petal fabric #1, cut 2 each of templates J and K, and 1 each of templates I and Ir.
- ✂ From petal fabric #2, cut 2 each of templates A and J.
- ✂ From petal fabric #3, cut 1 each of templates I and Ir.
- ✂ From flower-center fabric, cut 2 of template A.

For the lower left and right sections, use templates A, B, C, H, Hr, M, Mr, T, and Tr.

- ✂ From the background fabric, cut 2 each of templates A, B, C, T, and Tr.
- ✂ From petal fabric #1, cut 1 each of templates H, Hr, M, and Mr.
- ✂ From flower-center fabric, cut 2 of template A.

Block Assembly

1. Make the 4 different 8" sections, following the piecing diagrams.
2. Assemble the block.
3. Appliqué bias strip or ribbon over the seam between the finished lower sections to represent a stem.

Bud and Leaf Block

8" x 16"

To make two finished 8" x 16" Bud and Leaf blocks for the wall hanging, follow the cutting and block assembly directions below.

Cutting

For the upper left and right sections, use templates A, B, FF, I, and Ir.

- ✂ From background fabric, cut 4 of template FF and 8 of template A.
- ✂ From dark fabric, cut 4 of template B.
- ✂ From medium fabric, cut 2 each of templates I and Ir.
- ✂ From light fabric, cut 2 each of templates I and Ir.

For the lower left and right sections, use templates A, E, FF, G, Gr, I, and Ir.

✂ From the background fabric, cut 4 of template FF, 3 each of templates G and Gr, and 2 of template E.

✂ From green fabric, cut 2 of template A and 1 each of templates I and Ir.

Block Assembly

1. Make the 4 different 8" sections, following the piecing diagrams.
2. Appliqué bias strip or ribbon over the seam line as shown in piecing diagram for lower left and right sections.
3. Assemble the two 8" x 16" blocks.

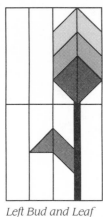

Left Bud and Leaf Blocks, 8" x 18"

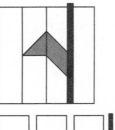

Upper Section of Left Bud & Leaf Block

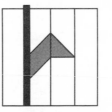

Lower Section of Left Bud & Leaf Block

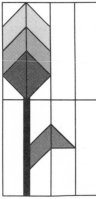

Right Bud and Leaf Blocks, 8" x 18"

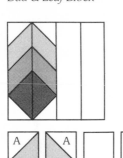

Upper Section of Right Bud & Leaf Block

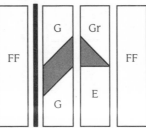

Lower Section of Right Bud & Leaf Block

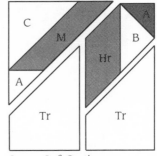

Lower Left Section

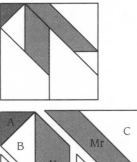

Lower Right Section

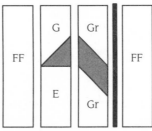

41

Karen's Iris Wall Hanging

64" x 48", plus borders

Karen Senet, a quilter who is a member of the American Iris Society, redesigned my Iris block after she saw my first attempt, and designed the Bud and Leaf block that appears in this wall hanging.

Materials

44"-wide fabric

2 yds. background fabric
¼ yd. each of 3 different fabrics (dark, medium, light)
    for flower petals and buds
¼ yd. fabric for flower centers
¾ yd. green fabric for leaves
2 yds. bias strip or narrow ribbon, ¼"–½" wide, for stems
Border fabrics as desired
3 yds. for backing
Batting and thread to finish

Directions

1. Following the diagrams, cut and piece:
   5 Iris blocks
   2 Bud and Leaf blocks
   6 Leaf #13 blocks (page 62)
   6 Leaf #14 blocks (page 62)
   6 Leaf #15 blocks (page 62)
   6 Leaf #16 blocks (page 62)
2. Assemble blocks into wall-hanging top, following assembly diagram.
3. Add borders as desired. (See page 12.)
4. Layer wall-hanging top with batting and backing. Quilt and bind as desired.

Karen's Iris Wall Hanging

Pansy

Pansies, with their funny little faces, are always a favorite in the garden. The color combinations found in natural pansies are practically unlimited; let your fancy roam free, but plan your colors so that the leaves are clearly defined.

Blocks like Pansy, with mirror-image sections, have many places where the seams must be carefully matched. This is one of the harder blocks in this book to piece, but still easy enough if you refer to the piecing diagram.

To make one finished 16"-square Pansy block, follow the cutting and block assembly directions below.

Cutting

For the upper left and right sections, use templates A, E, G, Gr, K, O, and U.

- ✂ From the background fabric, cut 6 of template A and 2 of template E.
- ✂ From petal fabric #1, cut 2 each of templates A and U.
- ✂ From petal fabric #2, cut 2 each of templates A and O and 1 each of templates G and Gr.
- ✂ From petal fabric #3, cut 2 of template K.

For the lower left and right sections, use templates A, B, E, G, Gr, I, Ir, L, Lr, and P.

- ✂ From the background fabric, cut 2 of template E and 4 of template A.
- ✂ From petal fabric #2, cut 2 of template P.
- ✂ From petal fabric #3, cut 4 of template B and 1 each of templates G, Gr, I, and Ir.
- ✂ From petal fabric #4, cut 1 each of templates G, Gr, I, Ir, L, and Lr.
- ✂ From flower-center fabric, cut 2 each of template B.

Block Assembly

1. Make the 4 different 8" sections, following the piecing diagrams.
2. Assemble the block.

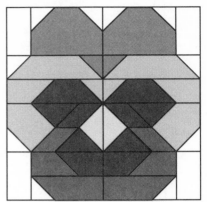

16" Pansy Block

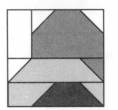

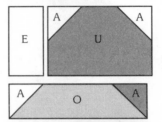

Upper Left Section

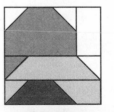

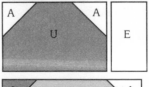

Upper Right Section

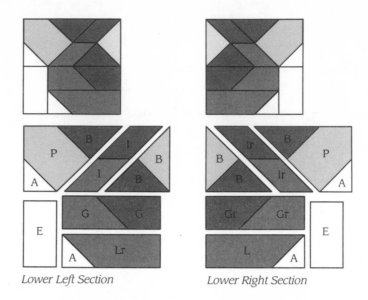

Lower Left Section   Lower Right Section

Stained-Glass Pansy Wall Hanging

28" x 52"

Outlining the different color groups with dark-colored narrow bias strip or ribbon gives this project a beautiful stained-glass effect. Appliqué by hand over the seam lines after the entire top is assembled. (I have also done the bias appliqué after the backing and batting are basted together with the top, so that the stitches can go all the way through to the backing and create quilt lines in themselves. If you do no further quilting of the flower blossoms, this method puffs them up a little and gives a pleasing effect.)

Materials

44"-wide fabric

½ yd. background fabric
¼ yd. each of 4 different fabrics for flower petals
¼ yd. fabric for flower centers
1½ yds. green fabric for leaves, borders, and binding
12 yds. bias strip or narrow ribbon, ¼"–½" wide
1⅔ yds. for backing
Batting and thread to finish

Directions

1. From the green fabric, cut:
   2 strips, 2½" x 48½", for side borders
   2 strips, 2½" x 28½", for top and bottom borders
2. Following the diagrams, cut and piece:
   3 Pansy blocks
   6 Leaf #12 blocks (page 61)
3. Assemble blocks and borders as shown in the diagram.
4. Layer wall-hanging top with batting and backing. Quilt and bind as desired.

Stained-Glass Pansy Wall Hanging

Bed of Pansies Quilt

84" x 100"

Materials

44"-wide fabric

3 yds. background fabric
¾ yd. each of 4 different fabrics for flower petals
½ yd. fabric for flower centers
3 yds. dark green fabric for leaves, borders, and binding
7 yds. for backing
Batting and thread to finish

Directions

1. From the dark green fabric, cut:
   2 strips, 2½" x 84½", for top and bottom borders
   2 strips, 2½" x 96½", for side borders
2. Following the diagrams on pages 43 and 44, cut and piece:
   20 Pansy blocks
   40 Leaf #12 blocks (page 61)
3. Assemble completed blocks, following quilt diagram. Add side borders; add top and bottom borders.
4. Layer quilt top with batting and backing. Quilt and bind as desired.

Bed of Pansies Quilt

Poinsettia

Bright red poinsettias with their yellow centers are Christmas favorites. This design was first published in the Christmas 1990 issue of Quilt World *magazine, which is edited by Sandra Hatch. Sandra was one of the first of my friends to ask me to share my quilt designs.*

The Poinsettia block could be made with all red petals and a yellow center, but I like to make one of the flower's two B pieces dark green to look like the corner of a leaf peeking from behind the flower.

To make one finished 16"-square Poinsettia block, follow the cutting diagram and block assembly directions below.

16" Poinsettia Block

8" Poinsettia Block

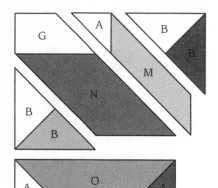

Piecing Diagram

Cutting

Use templates A, B, G, M, N, and O.

✂ From the background fabric, cut 8 each of templates A and B and 4 of template G.

✂ From 4 different red fabrics, cut 4 each of templates B, M, N, and O, using **1** fabric for each template.

✂ From yellow fabric, cut 4 of template A for center.

✂ From green fabric, cut 4 of template B.

Block Assembly

1. Make four 8"-square Poinsettia sections, following the piecing diagram.

2. Assemble block, rotating each section one-quarter turn around the A center pieces.

Poinsettia Wall Hanging

24" x 60"

The Poinsettia wall hanging adorns our back door during the Christmas season, a bright spot in our little back hallway. The top flower of the wall hanging is made like the block shown in the piecing diagram. The middle flower is reversed. The bottom flower is like the top one except that the position of the green leaf piece (template B) has been changed.

Materials

44"-wide fabric

1½ yds. background fabric
1 yd. green fabric for leaves, border, and binding
¼ yd. each of 4 red fabrics for flower petals
⅛ yd. yellow fabric for flower centers
1¾ yds. for backing
Batting and thread to finish

Directions

1. From background fabric, cut:
   2 strips, 2½" x 52½", for side sashing
   2 strips, 2½" x 20½", for top and bottom sashing
   2 strips, 2½" x 16½", for inner sashing between blocks
2. Following the diagrams, cut and piece:
   2 Poinsettia blocks (1 with green piece position changed as shown in diagram)
   1 reversed Poinsettia block
3. From background fabric, cut 4 of template A and 38 of template B. From dark green fabric, cut 4 of template A and 38 of template B. Use these pieces to make the pieced border as shown in the diagrams.
4. Assemble pieced blocks and inner sashing, referring to diagram. Add side sashing pieces; then add top and bottom sashing pieces. Add pieced borders on sides; add pieced borders to top and bottom.
5. Layer wall-hanging top with batting and backing. Quilt and bind as desired.

Poinsettia Wall Hanging

Pieced Bottom Border Showing Corner Piecing

Primrose

Dark points edge the Primrose design to represent the tips of leaves. The coloring of this design is among the simplest in this book; in order to introduce visual interest, make each of the flowers from a slightly different fabric in the same color family.

To make one finished 16"-square Primrose block, follow the cutting and block assembly directions below.

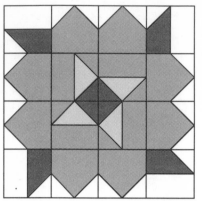
16" Primrose Block

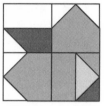
8" Primrose Block

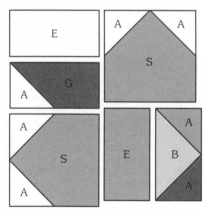
Piecing Diagram

Cutting

Use templates A, B, E, G, and S.

- ✄ From the background fabric, cut 4 of template E and 20 of template A.
- ✄ From petal fabric #1, cut 8 of template S, 4 of template E, and 4 of template A.
- ✄ From petal fabric #2, cut 4 of template B.
- ✄ From flower-center fabric, cut 4 of template A.
- ✄ From green leaf fabric, cut 4 of template G.

Block Assembly

1. Make four 8"-square sections, following the piecing diagram.
2. Assemble block, rotating each section one-quarter turn around the A center pieces.

Primrose Table Runner

20" x 92"

The table runner has two reversed blocks to add interest to the design. Blocks may be added to or subtracted from the table runner to make it the correct length for your holiday table. Any 16"-square block may be substituted for the Primrose block in this project.

Materials

44"-wide fabric

1 yd. background fabric
½ yd. petal fabric #1
¼ yd. petal fabric #2
¼ yd. fabric for flower centers
¼ yd. green fabric for leaf tips
½ yd. for binding
1½ yds. for backing
Batting and thread to finish (Use very thin batting for a table runner.)

Directions

1. Following the diagrams, cut and piece:
   3 Primrose blocks
   2 reversed Primrose blocks
2. From background fabric, cut:
   6 strips, 2½" x 20½", for sashing between flower blocks
   10 strips, 2½" x 16½", for sashing at sides of table runner

3. Assemble blocks and sashing strips into table runner, following diagram at right.
4. Layer runner top with batting and backing. Quilt and bind as desired.

Primrose Quilt with Leafy Border

72" x 90"

Any 16" flower block could be used with this leafy border. Other leaf blocks can also be used for a border, but this one seems particularly graceful.

Materials

44"-wide fabric

4 yds. background fabric
3 yds. green for leaves and binding
1½ yds. petal fabric #1
½ yd. petal fabric #2
¼ yd. fabric for flower centers
6 yds. for backing
Batting and thread to finish

Directions

1. From background fabric, cut:
   5 strips, 2½" x 72½", for horizontal sashing
   16 strips, 2½" x 16½", for in between flower blocks
   8 strips, 2½" x 8½", for in between groups of leaf blocks
2. Following the diagrams, cut and piece:
   12 Primrose blocks (some could be reversed if you prefer)
   16 Leaf #10 blocks (page 61)
   16 Leaf #11 blocks (page 61)
3. Assemble the quilt top in horizontal sections as shown in the assembly diagram below.
4. Layer quilt top with batting and backing. Quilt and bind as desired.

Primrose Quilt with Leafy Border

Primrose Table Runner

Red, Red Rose

16"–Square Section of Red, Red Rose

Red, Red Rose is an exception to the 16" flower blocks in this book. It, too, is made of four identical sections rotated around a center, but in this case each section is 16" square, and the completed block is 32" x 32". Each section is pieced in strips.

This block is extremely easy to piece, but it is the most complicated design in this book in terms of color selection. Colors must be planned very carefully to shade from the center out—either from light to dark or vice versa. (Or, you may prefer to do as I did and cut out all the pieces for the block first and pin them to a sheet to work out exactly the shading that you want.)

The AA template in the corner blocks is an exception to the 2" grid, but it makes everything come out right when the ½"-wide stem is added to the inside of the pieced border strips.

To make one finished 32"-square Red, Red Rose block, follow the cutting and block assembly directions below. Choose three closely related shades of green for the leaves (fabrics #1–#3). For the petals, choose two light fabrics, three medium fabrics, and two dark fabrics of the preferred color.

Cutting

Use templates A, B, D, F, G, Gr, H, Hr, Ir, K, L, LL, and O.

✂ From background fabric, cut 4 strips, 2½" x 16½", 12 of template B, 8 each of templates A and Gr, and 4 each of templates F, G, and LL.

✂ From green fabric #1, cut 4 of template K.

✂ From green fabric #2, cut 4 each of templates K and Hr.

✂ From green fabric #3, cut 4 each of templates H and O.

Arranging the petal fabrics from lightest to darkest, cut the following:

✂ From flower-center fabric, cut 4 of template A.

✂ From petal fabric #1, cut 4 each of templates A and B.

✂ From petal fabric #2, cut 4 each of templates G, Ir, and K.

✂ From petal fabric #3, cut 8 of template B and 4 of template A.

✂ From petal fabric #4, cut 8 of template B and 4 of template D.

✂ From petal fabric #5, cut 8 of template K and 4 of template L.

✂ From petal fabric #6, cut 4 each of templates B, K, and Gr.

Block Assembly

1. Make four 16"-square Red, Red, Rose sections, following the piecing diagram.
2. Assemble the 32"-square block, rotating each section one-quarter turn around the A center pieces.

Red, Red Rose Wall Hanging

45" x 45"

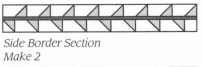

Pieced Sections for the Sides

Materials

44"-wide fabric

1½ yds. background fabric
¼ yd. each of 3 green fabrics for leaves and pieced borders
¼ yd. dark green fabric for stem in pieced border
⅛ yd. each of 2 light fabrics for rose
¼ yd. each of 3 medium fabrics for rose
¼ yd. each of 2 dark fabrics for rose
½ yd. for binding
1½ yds. for backing
Batting and thread to finish

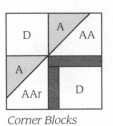

Corner Blocks

Directions

1. From the background fabric, cut:
   2 strips, 2½" x 41½", for outer side borders
   2 strips, 2½" x 45½", for outer top and bottom borders
   12 of template D, 4 of template AA, 4 of template AAr, 28 of template G, and 32 of template Gr for the pieced borders
2. From assorted green fabrics, cut 72 of template A for the pieced borders.
3. For the stem, cut from the dark green:
   4 pieces, 1" x 32½", for the side sections of the pieced border
   4 pieces, each 1" x 3", and 4 pieces, each 1" x 2½", for the corner blocks
4. Following the diagrams, cut and piece one 32"-square Red, Red Rose block.
5. Assemble the pieced border sections as shown in the piecing diagrams, attaching the corner blocks to the top and bottom sections.
6. Assemble the wall hanging by adding the side borders to the center sections. Add the top and bottom pieced borders. Add the plain side strips. Finish by adding the top and bottom plain strips.
7. Layer the wall-hanging top with batting and backing. Quilt and bind as desired.

Side Border Section
Make 2

Top and Bottom Border Sections
Make 2

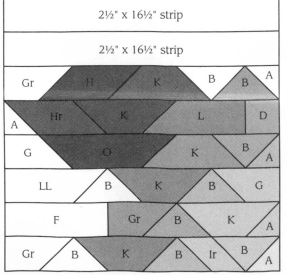

Piecing Diagram

Red, Red Rose Wall Hanging

51

Sunflower

16" Sunflower Block

8" Sunflower Section

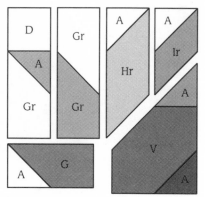

Piecing Diagram

Perhaps because I was Kansas-born and -bred, the Sunflower is my favorite of all these designs. The Field of Sunflowers wall hanging has the look of a hot summer day at the edge of a Kansas cornfield.

Note that in each section a Gr and A template are in the same color to represent a single petal; an I and A template also are in the same color. Careful attention to this detail will make a realistic-looking sunflower with four petals in each section.

To make one finished 16"-square Sunflower block, follow the cutting and block assembly directions below.

Cutting

Use templates A, D, G, Gr, Hr, Ir, and V.

✂ From background fabric, cut 12 of template A, 8 of template Gr, and 4 of template D.

✂ From flower-center fabric #1, cut 4 of template A.

✂ From flower-center fabric #2, cut 4 of template V.

✂ From petal fabric #1, cut 4 each of templates A and Ir.

✂ From petal fabric #2, cut 4 of template Hr.

✂ From petal fabric #3, cut 4 each of templates A and Gr.

✂ From petal fabric #4, cut 4 of template G.

Field of Sunflowers Wall Hanging

32" x 56", plus borders

Materials

44"-wide fabric

1½ yds. background fabric
¾ yd. green for stems and leaves
¼ yd. each of 6 different fabrics, including bright yellow, orange, and brown, for flower centers and petals
Border fabrics as desired
½ yd. for binding
1¾ yds. for backing
Batting and thread to finish

Directions

1. Following the diagrams, cut and piece:
   1 Sunflower block
   2 reversed Sunflower blocks
   2 Leaf #13 blocks (page 62)
   2 Leaf #14 blocks (page 62)
   7 Leaf #15 blocks (page 62)
   5 Leaf #16 blocks (page 62)
2. Assemble blocks into wall-hanging top, following assembly diagram.
3. Layer wall-hanging top with batting and backing. Quilt and bind as desired.

Field of Sunflowers Wall Hanging

Tall Tulip

Tall Tulip, 12" x 24"

This Tall Tulip block is 12" x 24" and is made in two sections. It is a different size and shape from the others in this book and cannot be used interchangeably in the settings like the others. Tall Tulip blocks can be arranged in straight rows with sashing between them for a nice quilt, but I used a staggered arrangement in the setting of my Tulip Garden quilt.

To make one finished 12" x 24" Tall Tulip block, follow the cutting and block assembly directions below.

Cutting

For the upper section, use templates A, B, J, N, Nr, O, T, and Tr.

- ✂ From background fabric, cut 4 of template A, 2 of template B, and 1 each of templates T and Tr.
- ✂ From fabric #1, cut 2 of template O and 1 each of templates N and Nr.
- ✂ From fabric #2, cut 2 each of templates A, B, and J.
- ✂ From fabric #3, cut 1 of template O.
- ✂ From fabric #4, cut 1 of template B.

For the lower section, use templates A, C, CC, M, Mr, MM, MMr, and Q.

- ✂ From background fabric, cut 4 of template C and 2 each of templates CC and Q.
- ✂ From green fabric, cut 2 of template A and 1 each of templates M, Mr, MM, and MMr.

For stem, cut 12½" strip of narrow bias or ribbon.

Block Assembly

1. Make the two 12" x 12" sections of the Tall Tulip, following the piecing diagrams.
2. Appliqué bias or narrow ribbon over the center seam of the lower section for stem.
3. Assemble the block.

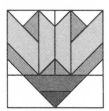

12" x 12" Upper Section

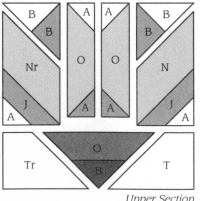

Upper Section

Tulip Garden Quilt

76" x 110"

Materials

44"-wide fabric

6 yds. background fabric
½ yd. each of 4 different bright-colored fabrics for flower petals
1 yd. green fabric for leaves
7 yds. bias strip or ribbon, ¼"–½" wide, for stems
2 yds. for outer border and binding (border is pieced)
6½ yds. for backing
Batting and thread to finish

Directions

1. From outside border fabric, cut enough 2½" strips to piece together:
   2 vertical border strips, 2½" x 106½"
   2 horizontal border strips, 2½" x 76½"
2. From background fabric, cut:
   6 vertical sashing strips, 2½" x 102½"
   2 horizontal sashing strips, 2½" x 72½"
   17 sashing strips, 2½" x 12½"
   2 rectangles, 12½" x 6½", as fill-in pieces at top of quilt
3. Following the diagrams, cut and piece:
   16 Tall Tulip blocks
   3 short Tall Tulip blocks (made by leaving out the lower pieces of the lower section—A, Q, MM, MMr, and CC)
   1 extra-tall Tall Tulip block (made by adding the special section, below right, to the bottom of a Tall Tulip block for the bottom center of the quilt)
4. Following quilt diagram, assemble pieced blocks into quilt top in vertical rows and attach vertical sashing strips.
5. Add top and bottom horizontal sashing.
6. Add the two side borders and finish by adding top and bottom borders.
7. Layer quilt top with batting and backing. Quilt and bind as desired.

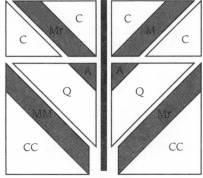

12" x 12" Lower Section

Lower Section

12" x 8" Section

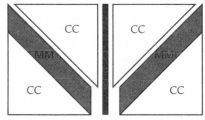

Special Section
Make 1

Tulip Garden Quilt

Flower Garden Sampler

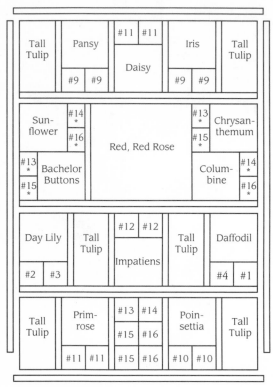

Assembly Diagram

The Flower Garden Sampler contains an example of each flower in this book and nearly all of the leaves. It was made using templates based on the 1" grid. (See pages 77–80.)

Flower Garden Sampler

42" x 57"

When made with the smaller templates (1" grid), the Red, Red Rose block around which the Flower Garden Sampler was planned is 16" square, and the remaining flower blocks are each 8" square.

Materials

44"-wide fabric

2 yds. background fabric
2 yds. fabric for sashing, borders, and binding
Assorted fabrics for flowers and leaves
1¾ yds. for backing (Be sure backing fabric is at least 44" wide; if it is less than 44" wide, buy 2½ yards.)
Batting and thread to finish

Directions

Use Templates with a 1" Grid on pages 77–80.

1. Following the piecing diagrams for each flower block, cut and piece:
   1 each of the flower blocks, except Tall Tulip
   6 Tall Tulip blocks
   1 block each Leaf #1, #2, #3, and #4
   2 blocks each Leaf #10 and #12
   4 blocks each Leaf #9 and Leaf #11
   3 blocks Leaf #13 (Omit the FF piece in 2 of these.*)
   3 blocks Leaf #14 (Omit the FF piece in 2 of these.*)
   4 blocks Leaf #15 (Omit the Gr-A-Gr-A row in 2 of these.*)
   4 blocks Leaf #16 (Omit the G-A-G-A row in 2 of these.*)
2. From the sashing and border fabric, cut:
   2 strips, 1½" x 42½", for top and bottom borders
   2 strips, 1½" x 55½", for side borders
   3 strips, 1½" x 40½", for horizontal sashing
   12 strips, 1½" x 12½", for vertical sashing
   2 strips, 1½" x 16½", for sashing on the sides of the Red, Red Rose block
3. Following the assembly diagram above for flower and leaf placement, assemble the blocks into 4 horizontal sections, adding vertical sashing strips between the blocks.
4. Join the sections into a wall-hanging top with horizontal sashing strips as shown.
5. Add side borders, then top and bottom borders.
6. Layer wall-hanging top with batting and backing. Quilt and bind as desired.

Flower Garden Sampler

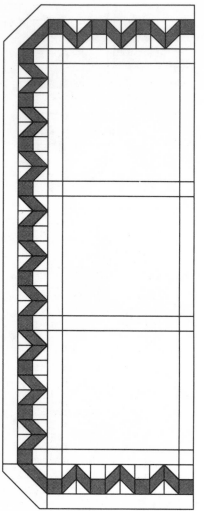

Construction Diagram for Scalloped Border

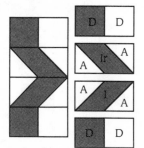

Piecing Diagram for Scalloped Border

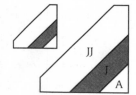

Piecing Diagram for Scalloped Border Corner

Scalloped Border for Blue and White Sampler Quilt

If you wish to make the scalloped border shown on the Blue and White Sampler quilt (page 17), use the piecing diagram, below left. The number of units per side can be adjusted to whatever number of 16" blocks you have in your quilt, as long as there is 2" sashing between each block. If you do not use 2" sashing between the blocks, this border may not fit your quilt without adjustment.

Because the setting blocks in the corners of the sashing are made of the background fabric, they will not be obvious, and they are very useful for keeping the assembly of the sashing on the square.

Template JJ is a special template for making the slanted corner and is an exception to the 2" grid used for the templates in this book.

To make a Scalloped Border for a quilt that contains twelve 16"-square blocks, set the blocks in three rows of four blocks each, as in the Blue and White Sampler quilt, and follow the cutting and assembly directions below. (Refer to the diagram of the Blue and White Sampler quilt on page 5.) The yardage given is for the outer border only on a 72" x 90" quilt.

Materials
44"-wide fabric

3¼ yds. background fabric
1 yd. dark fabric

Cutting
Use templates A, D, I, Ir, J, and JJ.

From background fabric, cut:

- ✂ 2 strips, 2½" x 56½", for outer top and bottom borders
- ✂ 2 strips, 2½" x 74½", for outer side borders
- ✂ 4 of template JJ
- ✂ 46 of template D
- ✂ 108 of template A

From dark fabric, cut:

- ✂ 4 of template J
- ✂ 46 of template D
- ✂ 42 each of templates I and Ir

Directions
1. Assemble center of quilt top with sashing between each block and around the outside of the 12 blocks. Sashing strips to surround 16"-square pieced blocks are cut 2½" x 16½"; setting blocks are 2½" x 2½" (template D).
2. Assemble borders and 4 corner pieces, following piecing diagrams.
3. Attach side borders to quilt.
4. Attach corner sections to top and bottom borders and add to quilt.

Leaves
All the leaves are sized to be used with any of the flower blocks to create new and different projects.

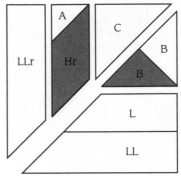

Leaf #1, 8" Block
Cutting
Use templates A, B, C, Hr, L, LL, LLr.

✂ From background fabric, cut 1 each of templates A, B, C, L, LL, and LLr.

✂ From leaf fabric, cut 1 each of templates B and Hr.

    Assemble block according to piecing diagram. Appliqué bias strip or narrow ribbon on assembled block to make the stem.

Leaf #1, Piecing Diagram

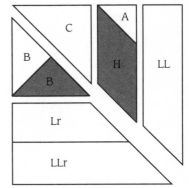

Leaf #2, 8" Block
Cutting
Use templates A, B, C, H, L, LL, and LLr.

✂ From background fabric, cut 1 each of templates A, B, C, L, LL, and LLr.

✂ From leaf fabric, cut 1 each of templates B and H.

    Assemble block, following piecing diagram. Appliqué bias strip or narrow ribbon on assembled block to make the stem.

Leaf #2, Piecing Diagram

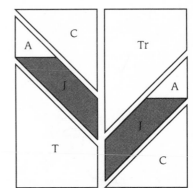

Leaf #3, 8" Block
Cutting
Use templates A, C, J, T, and Tr.

✂ From background fabric, cut 2 each of template A and C and 1 each of templates T and Tr.

✂ From leaf fabric, cut 2 of template J.

    Assemble block, following piecing diagram. Appliqué bias strip on assembled block to make the stem.

Leaf #3, Piecing Diagram

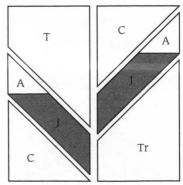

Leaf #4, 8" Block
Cutting
Use templates A, C, J, T, and Tr.

✂ From background fabric, cut 2 each of template A and C and 1 each of templates T and Tr.

✂ From leaf fabric, cut 2 of template J.

    Assemble block, following piecing diagram. Appliqué bias strip on assembled block to make the stem.

Leaf #4, Piecing Diagram

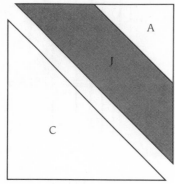

Leaf #5, Piecing Diagram

Leaf #5, 4" Block

Cutting

Use templates A, C, and J.

✂ From background fabric, cut 1 each of templates A and C.

✂ From leaf fabric, cut 1 of template J.

Assemble block, following piecing diagram.

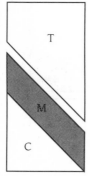

Leaf #6, Piecing Diagram

Leaf #6, 4" x 6" Block

Cutting

Use templates C, M, and T.

✂ From background fabric, cut 1 each of templates C and T.

✂ From leaf fabric, cut 1 of template M.

Assemble block, following piecing diagram.

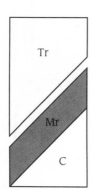

Leaf #7, Piecing Diagram

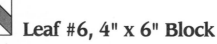

Leaf #7, 4" x 8" Block

Cutting

Use templates C, Mr, and Tr.

✂ From background fabric, cut 1 each of templates C and Tr.

✂ From leaf fabric, cut 1 of template Mr.

Assemble block, following piecing diagram.

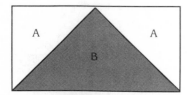

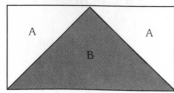

Leaf #8, Piecing Diagram

Leaf #8, 4" Block

Cutting

Use templates A and B.

✂ From background fabric, cut 4 of template A.

✂ From leaf fabric, cut 2 of template B.

Assemble block, following piecing diagram.

Leaf #9, 8" Block

Cutting

Use templates A, LL, LLr, and Q.

✂ From background fabric, cut 2 of template A and 1 each of templates LL and LLr.

✂ From leaf fabric, cut 2 of template Q.

Assemble block, following piecing diagram. Appliqué bias strip or narrow ribbon on assembled block to make the stem.

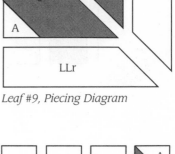
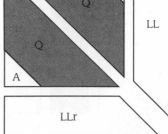

Leaf #9, Piecing Diagram

Leaf #10, 8" Block

Cutting

Use templates A, D, G, Hr, and K.

✂ From background fabric, cut 3 each of templates A and G and 1 each of templates D and K.

✂ From leaf fabric, cut 2 each of templates A and K and 1 of template Hr.

Assemble block, following piecing diagram.

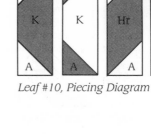

Leaf #10, Piecing Diagram

Leaf #11, 8" Block

Cutting

Use templates A, D, Gr, H, and K.

✂ From background fabric, cut 3 each of templates A and Gr and 1 each of templates D and K.

✂ From leaf fabric, cut 2 each of templates A and K and 1 of template H.

Assemble block, following piecing diagram.

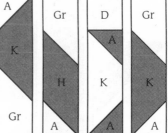

Leaf #11, Piecing Diagram

Leaf #12, 8" Block

Cutting

Use templates A, B, L, Lr, R, and Rr.

✂ From background fabric, cut 6 of template A and 1 each of templates L and Lr.

✂ From leaf fabric, cut 2 of template B and 1 each of templates R and Rr.

Assemble block, following piecing diagram.

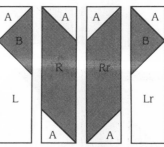

Leaf #12, Piecing Diagram

1.

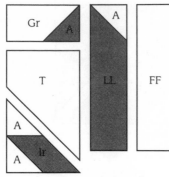

Leaf #13, Piecing Diagram

Leaf #13, 8" Block

Cutting

Use templates A, FF, Gr, Ir, LL, and T.

- ✄ From background fabric, cut 3 of template A and 1 each of templates FF, Gr, and T.
- ✄ From leaf fabric, cut 1 each of templates A, Ir, and LL.

  Assemble block, following piecing diagram.

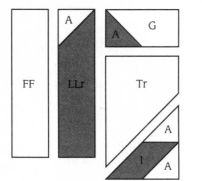

Leaf #14, Piecing Diagram

Leaf #14, 8" Block

Cutting

Use templates A, FF, G, I, LLr, and Tr.

- ✄ From background fabric, cut 3 of template A and 1 each of templates FF, G, and Tr.
- ✄ From leaf fabric, cut 1 each of templates A, I, and LLr.

  Assemble block, following piecing diagram.

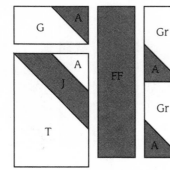

Leaf #15, Piecing Diagram

Leaf #15, 8" Block

Cutting

Use templates A, FF, G, Gr, J, and T.

- ✄ From background fabric, cut 1 each of templates A, G, and T and 2 of template Gr.
- ✄ From leaf fabric, cut 3 of template A and 1 each of templates FF and J.

  Assemble block, following piecing diagram.

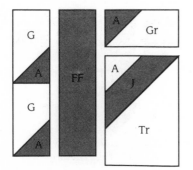

Leaf #16, Piecing Diagram

Leaf #16, 8" Block

Cutting

Use templates A, FF, G, Gr, J, and Tr.

- ✄ From background fabric, cut 1 each of templates A, Gr, and Tr and 2 of template G.
- ✄ From leaf fabric, cut 3 of template A and 1 each of templates FF and J.

  Assemble block, following piecing diagram.

TEMPLATES

Templates with a 2" Grid (pages 64–76)

With the exception of the Flower Garden Sampler, all the designs in this book are described, directions given, and fabric requirements estimated presuming the use of the 2" grid. Inexperienced quilters will find these pieces easy to work with, and the straight seams make these suitable projects for beginners.

Templates with a 1" Grid (pages 77–80)

A set of smaller templates is also included in this book. These can be used to make the Flower Garden Sampler as described in the directions for that project. Intermediate quilters should have no problem with a project using these smaller templates.

When making a crib quilt or wall hanging, you may prefer the smaller templates, but remember that they produce a finished flower block only 8" square, so you will need to make more blocks for each project.

Making Wooden Templates

When I plan to make an entire quilt top using the same pieced block over and over, I want templates that are sturdy enough so that I can cut out all the pieces with my rotary cutter without destroying the templates.

I carefully draw each template on graph paper (or in the case of this book, simply copy the templates on a good copier that reproduces at exactly 100 percent of the original size) and cut them out, leaving an additional half-inch or so of paper around the template. In my husband's workshop, I glue the paper templates onto scraps of three-ply plywood that is about ¼" thick.

After the glue dries, I cut carefully along the outside edges of the template with a band saw. Anyone who can use a sewing machine can use a band saw. In fact, your "sewing eye" and steady hand may make you a more accurate band sawyer than the guy who bought the saw.

Sand the edges lightly to get rid of any splinters, and your wooden templates are ready to use over and over again. Because the same templates are often used in many patterns, I keep all my wooden templates, marked with size, and rummage through my template collection to find those I need for a project.

If you do not have access to your own band saw, or to the band saw of someone whom you could cajole into making templates for you, trace the templates onto the material that has worked best for you in the past—plastic, cardboard, or whatever—and use the templates carefully with your rotary cutter. All the edges are straight, which will make this easy.

These full-size templates have ¼" seam allowances printed with a grid pattern to show the proper grain line of the fabric.

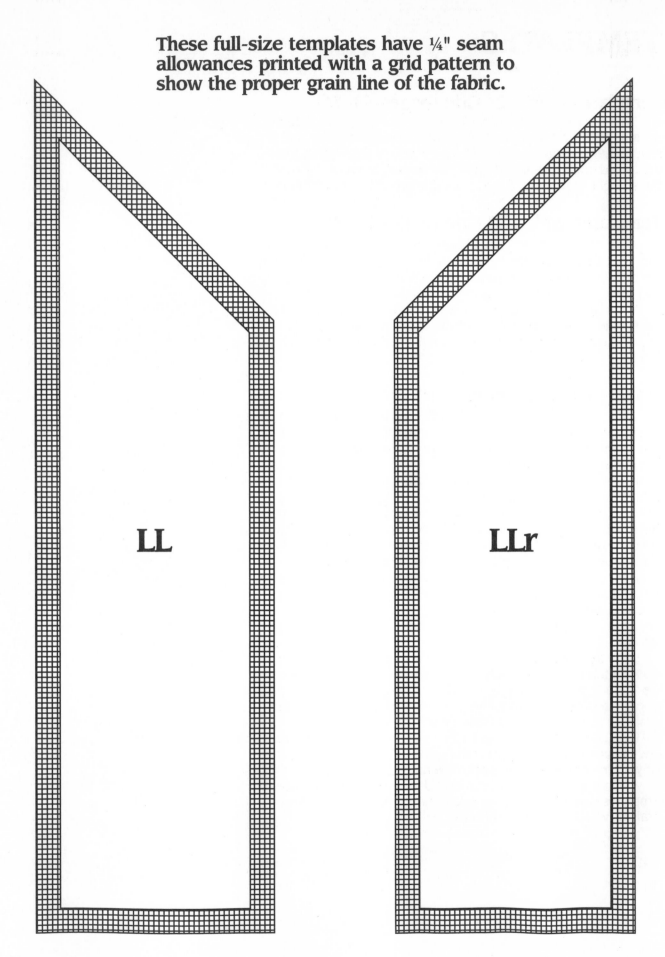

LL

LLr

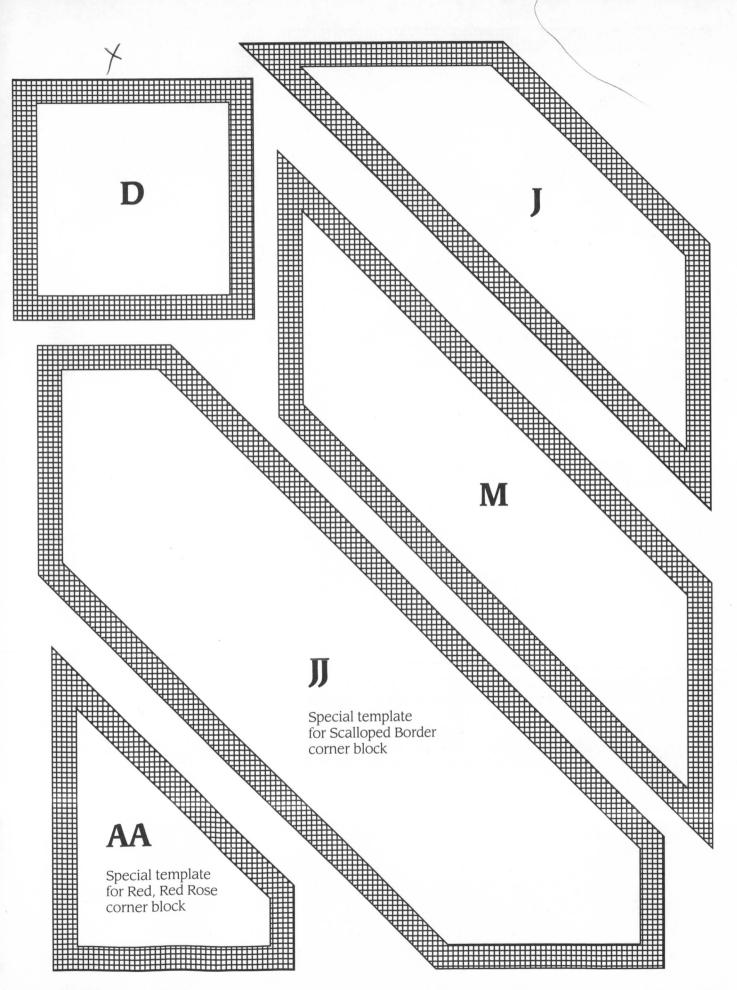

D

J

M

JJ

Special template
for Scalloped Border
corner block

AA

Special template
for Red, Red Rose
corner block

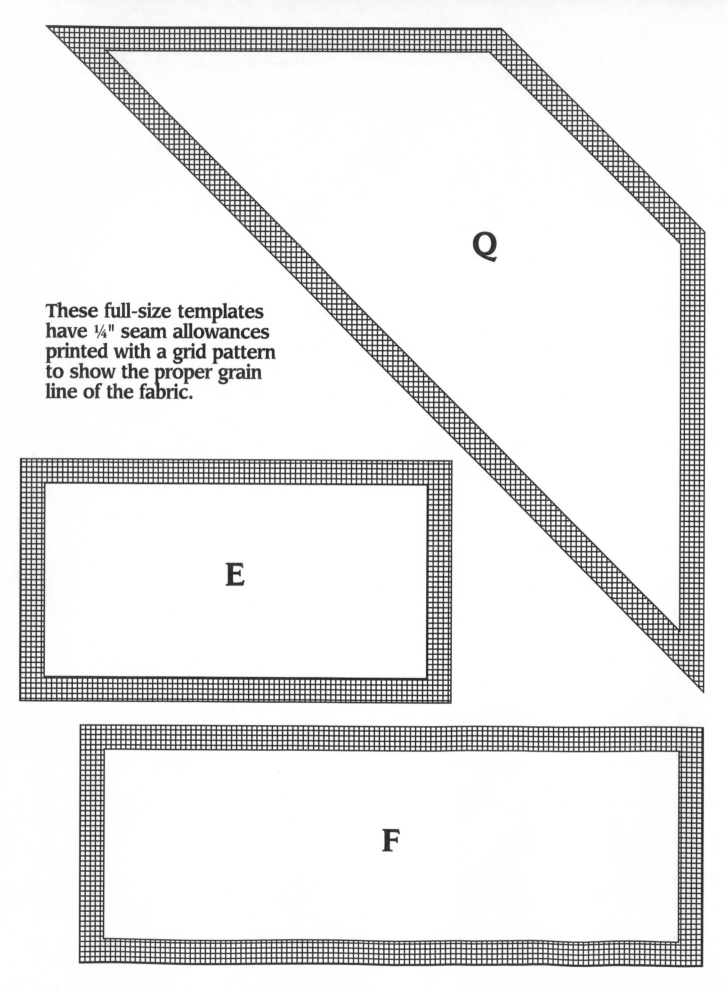

These full-size templates have ¼" seam allowances printed with a grid pattern to show the proper grain line of the fabric.

Q

E

F

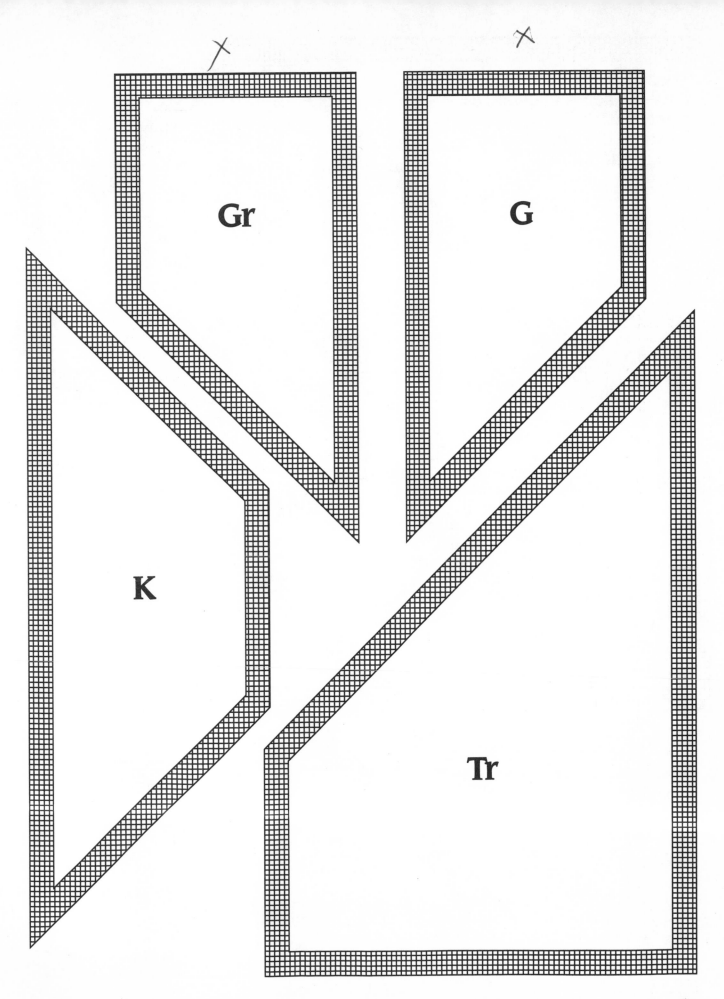

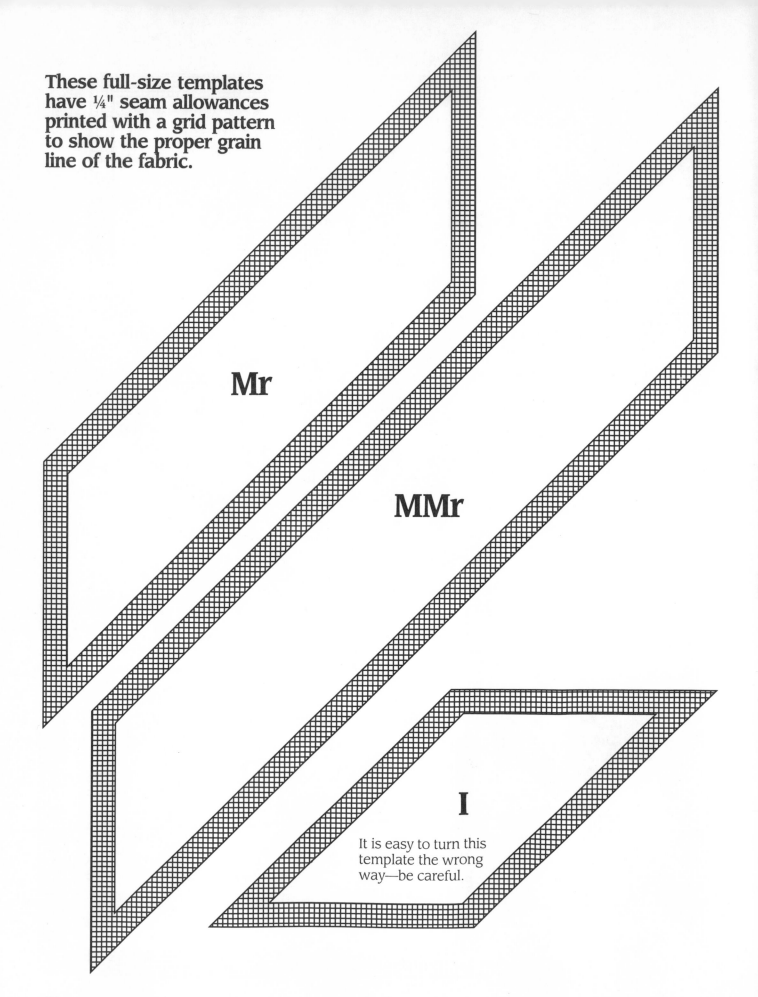

These full-size templates have ¼" seam allowances printed with a grid pattern to show the proper grain line of the fabric.

Mr

MMr

I

It is easy to turn this template the wrong way—be careful.

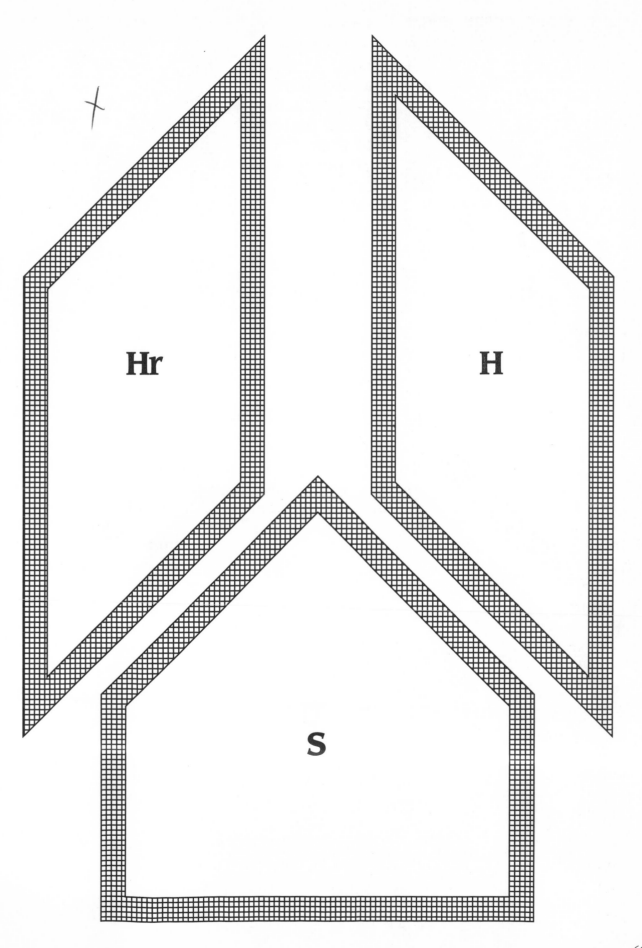

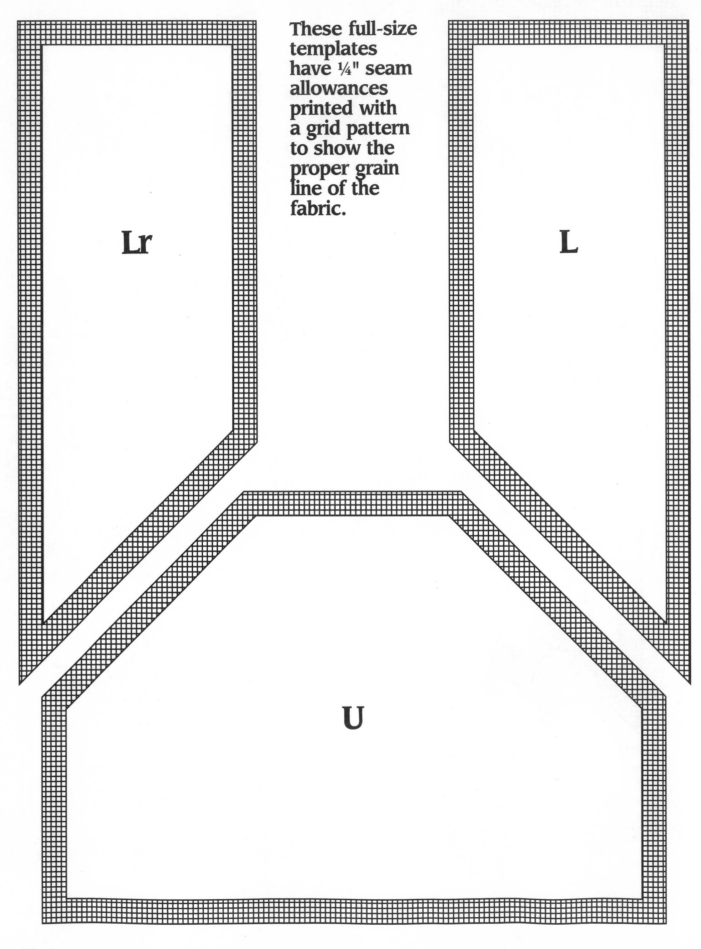

These full-size templates have ¼" seam allowances printed with a grid pattern to show the proper grain line of the fabric.

Lr

L

U

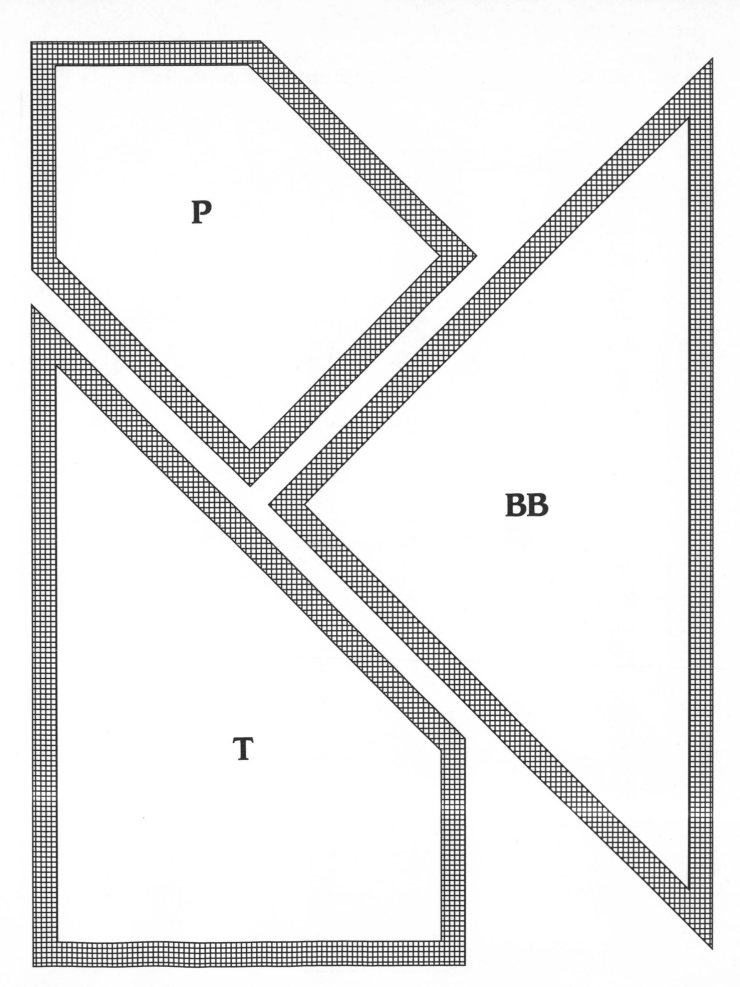

P

BB

T

These full-size templates have ¼" seam allowances printed with a grid pattern to show the proper grain line of the fabric.

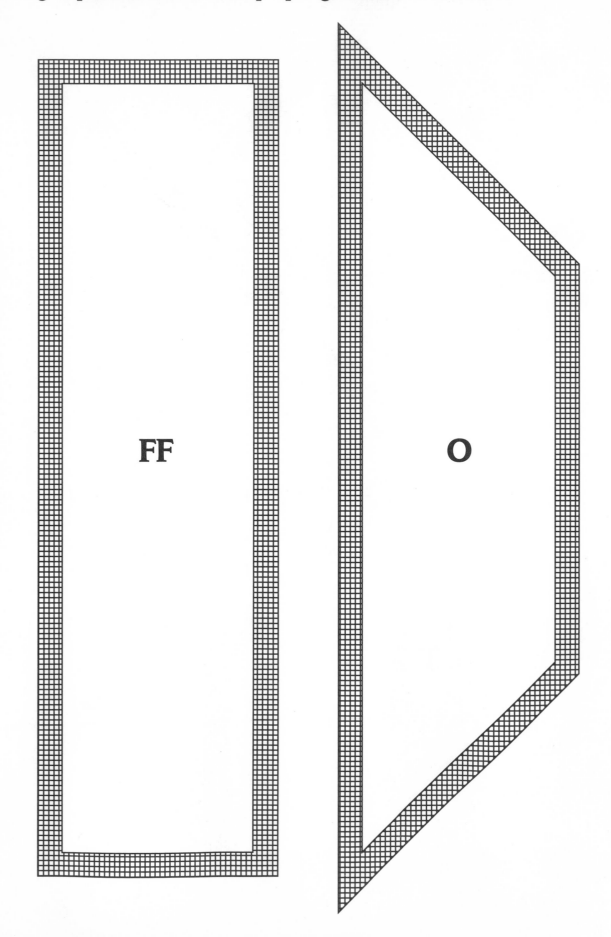

FF

O

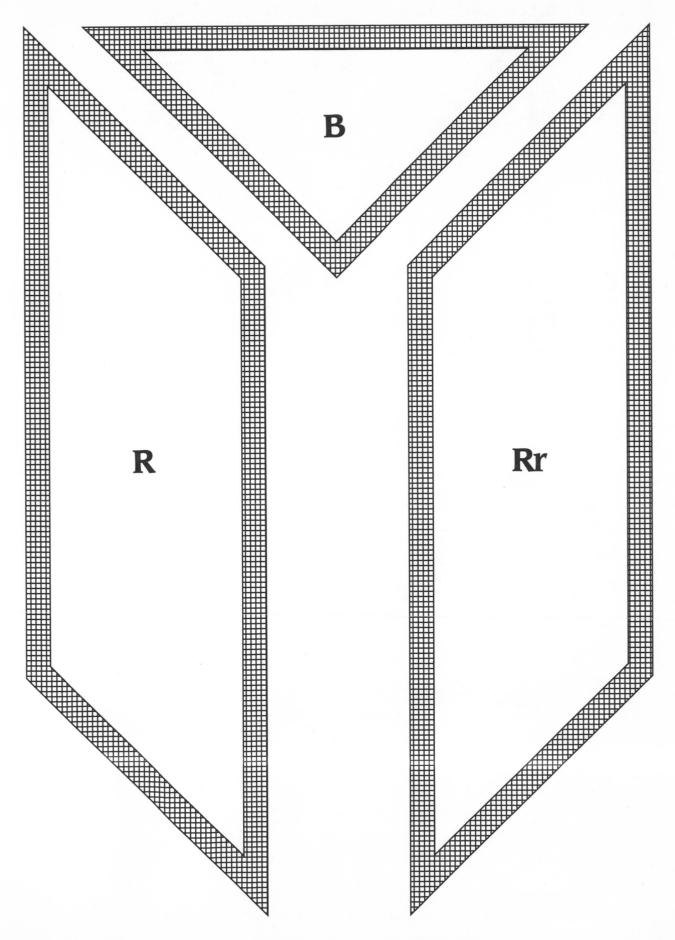

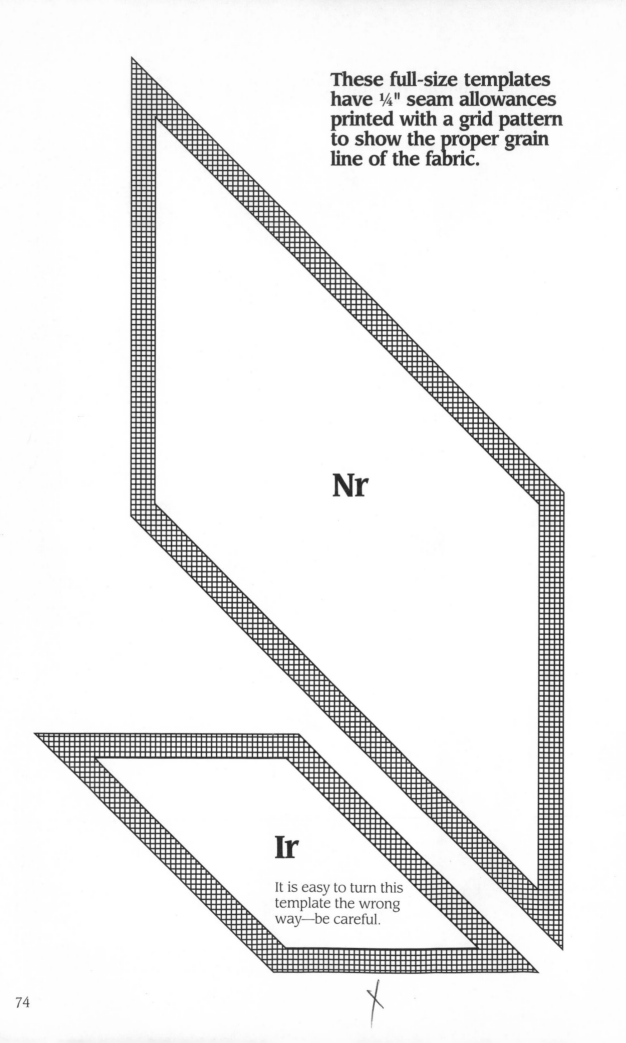

These full-size templates have ¼" seam allowances printed with a grid pattern to show the proper grain line of the fabric.

Nr

Ir

It is easy to turn this template the wrong way—be careful.

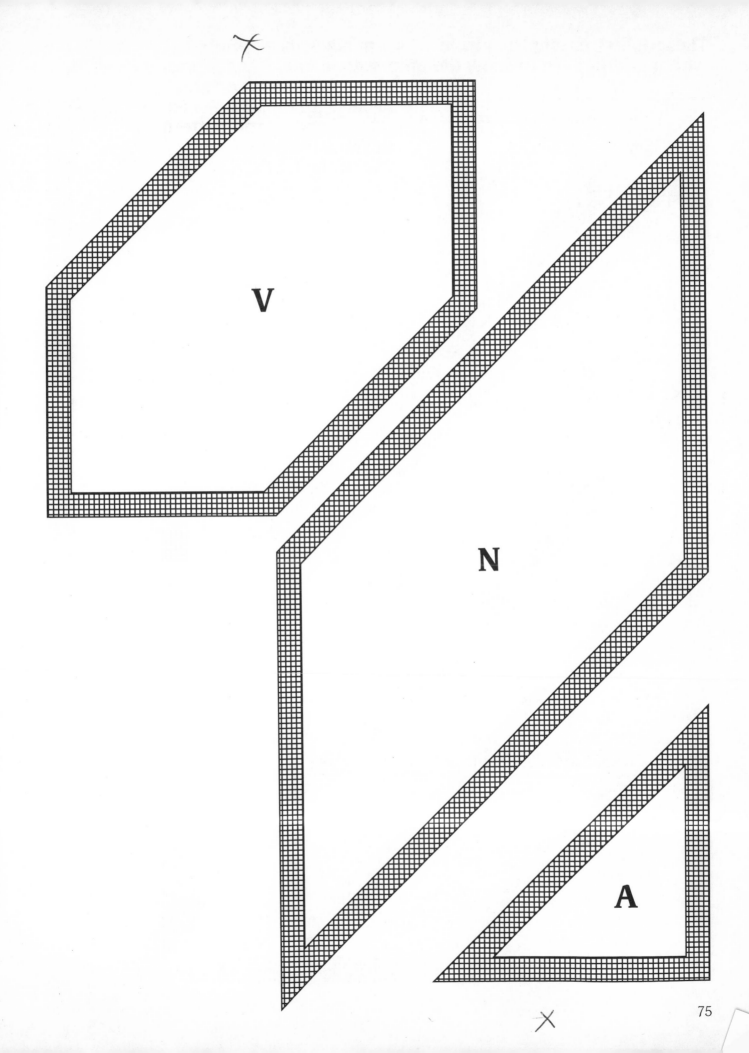

V

N

A

These full-size templates have ¼" seam allowances printed with a grid pattern to show the proper grain line of the fabric.

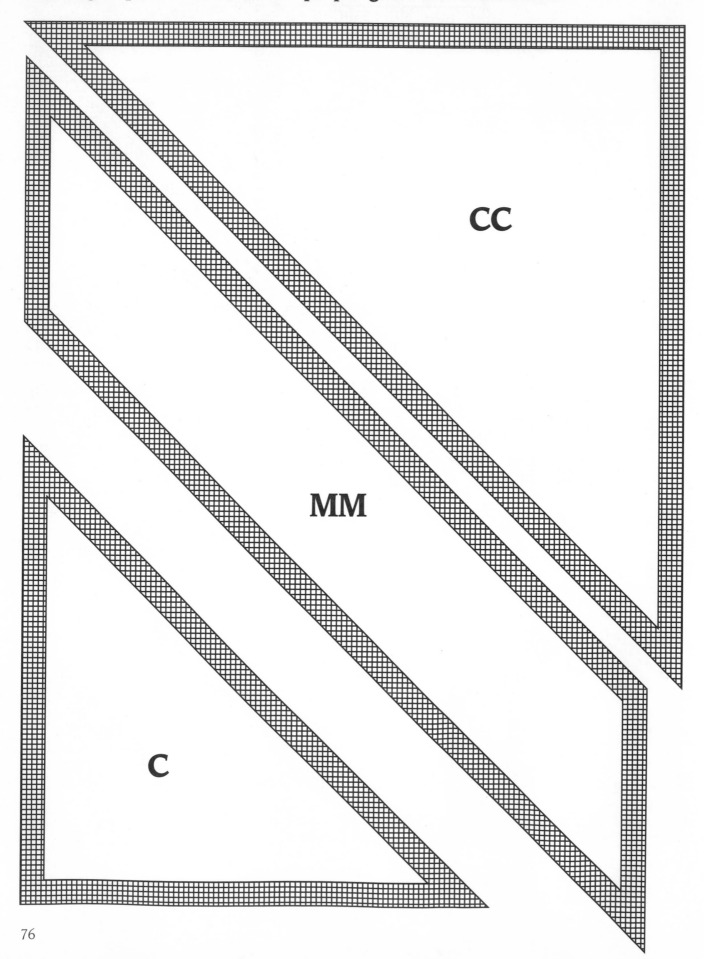

These small templates are based on a 1" grid.

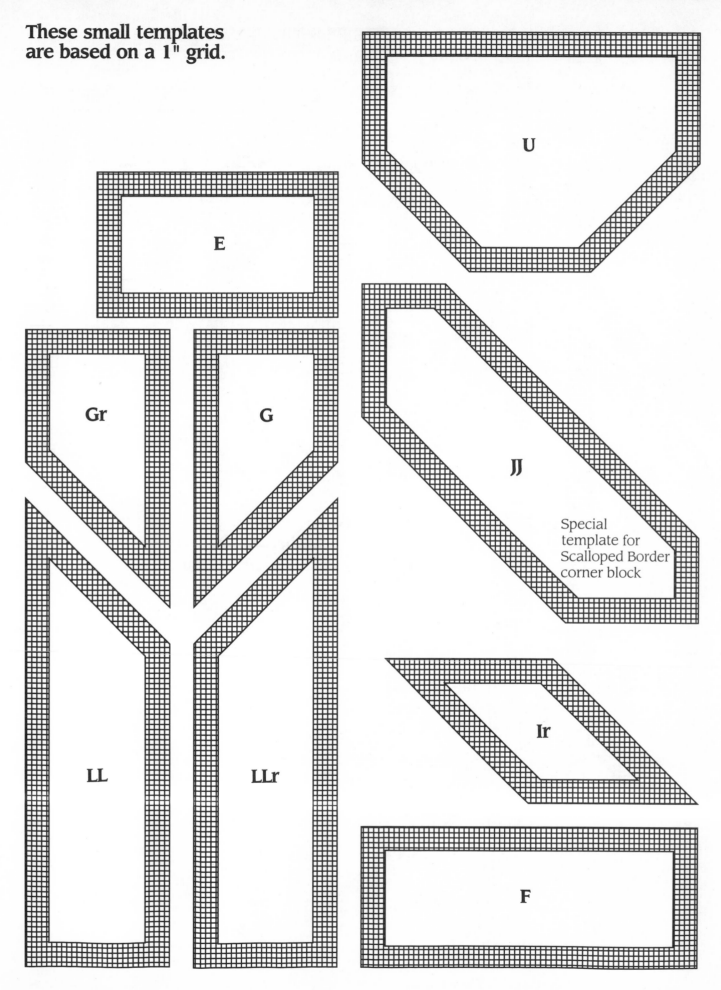

U

E

Gr

G

JJ

Special
template for
Scalloped Border
corner block

LL

LLr

Ir

F

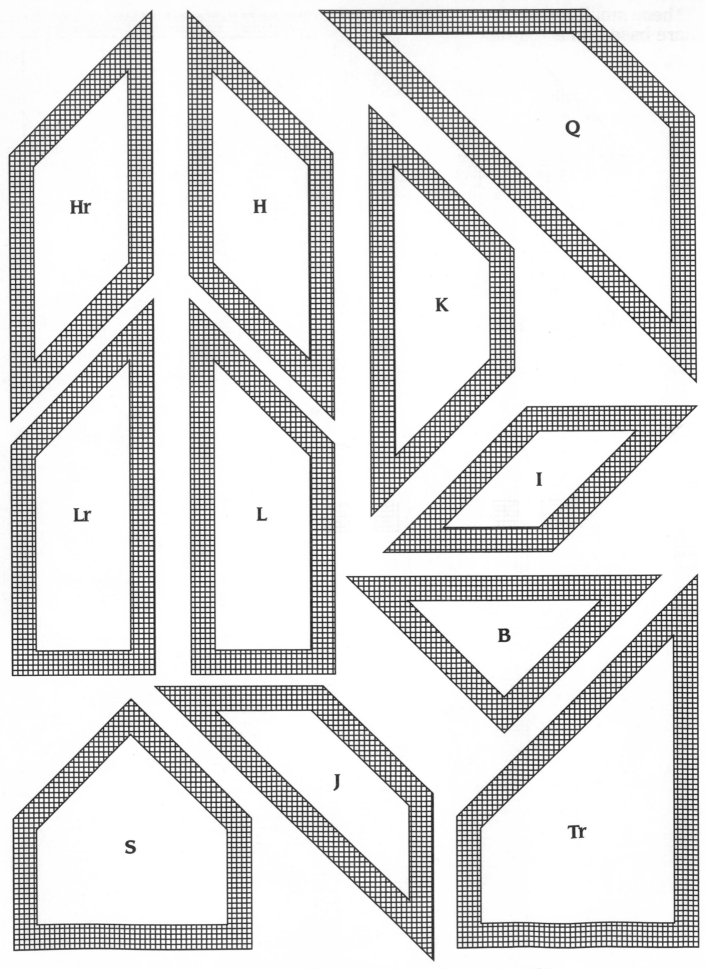

These small templates are based on a 1" grid.

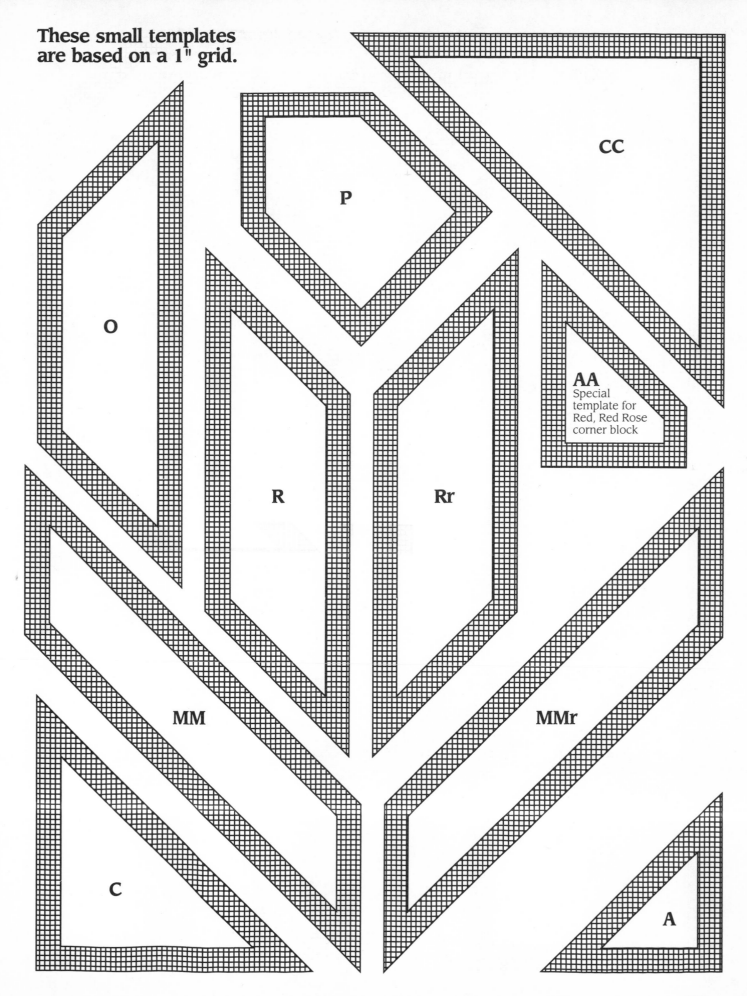

These small templates are based on a 1" grid.

CC

P

O

AA
Special template for Red, Red Rose corner block

R

Rr

MM

MMr

C

A

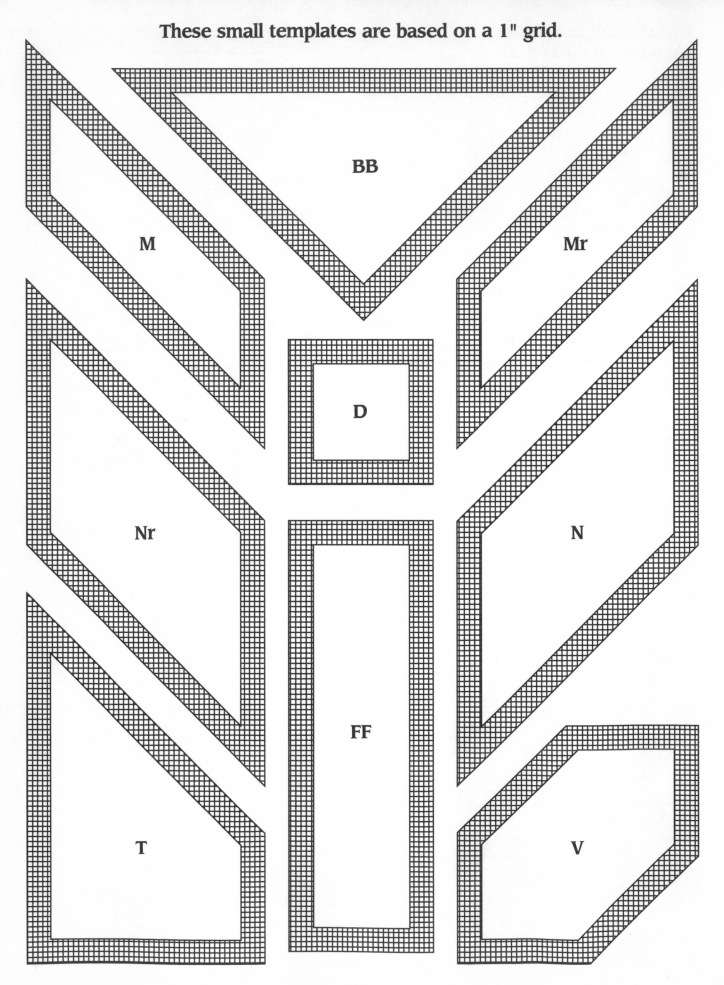